THE SHIRLEY LETTERS FROM CALIFORNIA MINES IN 1851-52

Being a Series of Twenty-three Letters from
DAME SHIRLEY

(Mrs. Louise Amelia Knapp Smith Clappe)

To her Sister in Massachusetts
and now Reprinted from the
Pioneer Magazine
of 1854-55

with
Synopses of the Letters, a Foreword,
and many Typographical
and other Corrections
and Emendations, by

THOMAS C. RUSSELL

Together with "An Appreciation" by
Mrs. M. V. T. Lawrence

ILLUSTRATED

SAN FRANCISCO
Printed by THOMAS C. RUSSELL,
at his Private Press
1734 Nineteenth Avenue
1922

Dame Shirley, the Writer of these Letters
An Appreciation

Being a Paper prepared by
Mrs. Mary Viola Tingley Lawrence

to be read before a San Francisco literary society on
Mrs. Louise Amelia Knapp Smith Clappe
(Dame Shirley)

The Shirley Letters, written in the pioneer days of 1851 and 1852, were hailed throughout the country as the first-born of California literature. Mrs. Clappe, their author, was the one woman who depicted that era of romantic life, dipping her pen into a rich personal experience, and writing with a clarity and beauty born of an alert comprehensive mind and a rare sense of refinement and character.

The Letters had been written to a loved sister in the East, but Ferdinand C. Ewer, a *littérateur* of San Francisco, a close friend, fell upon them by chance, and, realizing their historic value, urged that they be published in the Pioneer, of which he was editor. These Shirley Letters, thus published, brought the new West to the wondering East, and showed to those who had not made the venture, the courage, the fervor, the beauty, the great-heartedness, that made up life in the new El Dorado. Shirley's sympathetic Interpretation of their tumultuous experience cheered the Argonauts by throwing before their eyes the drama in which they were unconsciously the swash-buckling, the tragic, or the romantic actors, and helped to crystallize the growing love for the new land, which love turned fortune and adventure seekers into home-makers and empire-builders.

This quickly recognized author became the leader of the first *salon* the Golden West ever knew, and one of the foremost influences in California's social and intellectual life, by force of a high intelligence and a heart and soul that were a noble woman's.

Louise Amelia Knapp Smith Clappe came to light in Elizabeth, New Jersey, in 1819. Her father, Moses Smith, was a man of high scholarly attainment, and by her mother, Lois Lee, she could claim an equally gifted ancestry, and a close kinship with Julia Ward Howe. As a young girl, together with several brothers and sisters, she was left parentless, but there was a comfortable estate, and a faithful guardian, the Hon. Osman Baker, a Member of Congress I believe, who saw to it that they received the very best mental and physical training. Shirley was educated at Amherst and Charlestown, Massachusetts, and at Amherst was the family home.

At that day the epistolary art was a finished accomplishment, and in childhood she evidenced a ready use of the quill pen. Later on, she maintained correspondence with brilliant minds, who challenged her to her best. At the same time she was pursuing her English studies, to which were added French, German, and Italian. She had but little time for the trivial social amenities, but her frequent missives from her relatives, the Lees and Wards of New York City and Boston, and her enjoyable visits to their gay homes, broke the strain of mental grind, and kept her in touch with the fashionable world. Her communications in the forties disclose a relation to men and women of culture, whose letters are colorful of people, places, and events, and through them we reach an intimate inside of her own self. Those faded, musty-smelling epistles, with pressed flowers, from an old attic, reveal a rich kind of distinct and charming personalities.

Shirley, small, fair, and golden-haired, was not physically strong, and her careful guardian often ordered a change of climate. Sometimes she sojourned in the South. In her migrations she might employ a carriage, or venture on a canal-boat, but usually the stage-coach carried her. It was on one of those bits of travel that she met Mr. A. H. Everett of Massachusetts, a brother of Edward Everett, a noted author, and popular throughout the country as a lecturer. He had been chargé d'affaires in the Netherlands, and minister to Spain. An intimate relationship, chiefly by correspondence, was established between this gifted girl and this brilliant gentleman. His long letters from Louisiana sometimes were written wholly in French. From Washington, D.C., he writes that the mission of United States minister to a foreign court has been offered him, but it fails to tempt him away from his life of letters. However, later on, it comes about that he accepts the mission of United States commissioner to the more alluring China, and his long letters to her from there, as they had been from other foreign lands, were most entertaining. This rare man grows to be very fond of his young and brilliant correspondent, and signs himself, "Yours faithfully and affectionately." But he was well on in years, and she looks upon him more as a father than as a suitor, and he so understands it. He commits himself enough to say how much it would be to him to have her near him as an attachée, and when she hints of her engagement to a young physician, he jealously begs to know every detail concerning the happy man.

Shirley married Dr. Fayette Clappe, and in 1849, with the spirit of romance and the fire of enthusiasm, the joyful young Argonauts set sail for California in the good ship Manilla.

They found the primitive San Francisco enthralling, but a fire swept away the new city, and tent-life was accepted as one of many picturesque experiences. Soon, however, the Doctor's shingle was again hung out.

Quickly buildings went up, and the little lady with golden curls to her waist went about, jostling the motley crowd of people, and finding concern in the active city front, in the gaudy shops, and in the open faro-banks with their exposed piles of nuggets and bags of gold-dust freshly dug from the earth.

There was the ever-beckoning to the hills of treasure, with their extravagant stories of adventure, but the professional man was anchored in the more prosy city, and buckled down to a commonplace existence. The exhilarating ozone from the ocean, the wind blowing over the vast area of sand, the red-flannel-shirted miner recklessly dumping out sacks of gold-dust with which to pay his board-bill or to buy a pair of boots, with maybe a nugget for Dr. Clappe when he eased a trivial pain,—all these thrills were calls to the gold-filled

Mother Earth. Finally, Dr. Clappe's ill-health drove him to the Feather River,—a high altitude, fifty miles from the summit of the Sierra Nevada, and the highest point of gold-diggings. There he soon recovered, and to her joy he wrote his wife to join him. And she had varying experiences in transit to the prospective home, which was at Rich Bar,—rich indeed, where a miner unearthed thirty-three pounds of gold in eight days, and others panned out fifteen hundred dollars in one wash of dirt.

The sojourn at the gold-camp in the summers and winters of 1851 and 1852, with its tremendous and varied incidents and experiences, was a compelling call to Shirley's facile pen. Here was her mine. Out of her brain, out of her soul, out of her heart of gold, out of her wealth of understanding of and love for her fellow-men, gratefully sprang those Shirley Letters that have enriched the field of letters, and, reaching beyond the grasp of worldly gain, have set her enduringly in the hearts of mankind.

Who can tell how far-reaching and inspiring were those illuminating pages, those vividly depicted scenes enacted on the crowded stages of the golden-lined bars of the famous Feather River! Bret Harte reads her graphic and pathetic account of the fallen woman and the desperate men being driven out of camp, and lo! we have the gripping tale of The Outcasts of Poker Flat; and from another of her recitals came the inspiration that set him to work on that entertaining story, The Luck of Roaring Camp. And her incidental mention of the pet frog hopping on the bar of the hotel, in the midst of a group of onlooking miners,—was it the setting for Mark Twain's Jumping Frog of Calaveras?

During their sojourn at Rich and Indian bars, Shirley and her husband became rich in experience. They folded their tent and left with depleted purse, but they had righteously invested their God-bestowed talents. There they had freely given the best of themselves; they were leaving the imperishable impress of high ideals.

Upon their return to San Francisco the couple rejoined delightful friends, and established a home. But reverses of fortune came, and Shirley found it necessary to put her accomplishments to the practical purpose of gaining a livelihood. By the advice of her friend Ferdinand

C. Ewer she entered the San Francisco public school department, where for long years she taught, notably in the high schools.

Shirley was small in build, with a thin face and a finely shaped head. Her limbs were perfect in symmetry. As a girl, doubtless she had claim to a delicate beauty. She now showed the wear and tear of her mountain experience, coupled with an accumulation of heart-breaking trouble. She gave prodigally of all her gifts. She interpreted life and its arts to all discerning pupils, and by the magic of her friendly intercourse won their confidence. Quick to discover any unusual promise in a pupil, she indefatigably and masterfully stirred up such a one to his or her best, sometimes with remarks of approval, or by censuring recreancy with stinging sarcasm, or with expressions of despair over infirmity of purpose. Some of such scholars, notably among them Charles Warren Stoddard, panned out gold in the field of letters. Many of her pupils, including myself, absorbed much of her wonderful help, and it grew into our subconsciousness and became a part of us. She was the long-time friend of Bret Harte, and from her he gathered a wealth of knowledge that served him well.

When Mr. Ewer was ordained in Grace Episcopal Church, San Francisco, Shirley became a member of his parish, and together with his wife she assisted him in the ministrations of good. Then this dependable friend, Dr. Ewer, was discovered, with the result that he was called to a church in New York at a salary of ten thousand dollars a year.

In addition to her daily teaching, Shirley, by request, established evening classes in art and literature, for men and women, and once a week she held her *salon*, drawing the best minds about her. She appreciated the privilege of having a home in Mr. John Swett's family, because of its intellectual atmosphere. Here scholarly notabilities from near and far were entertained, among them Emerson, Agassiz, and Julia Ward Howe.

Childless, Shirley took her niece, Genevieve Stebbins, and reared her from babyhood to a splendid womanhood. She contributed freely to entertainments for charity, by her Shakespearean readings and other recitations, and happily prepared whole parties for private theatricals. With such mental strain, she kept herself fit by Saturday outings, in which were graciously included some of her pupils. At times we went across the bay, in various directions, but oftenest we strove through the sand to the ocean beach, stopping here and there to botanize, and gather the sweet yellow and purple lupin, and to rest on the limbs of the scrub-oaks. On the beach we roasted potatoes and made coffee, and then ate ravenously. A happy gipsying it was, and she, the queen, forgot her cares. Not a pebble at our feet, nor a floating seaweed, nor a shell, nor a seal on the rock, but opened up an instructive talk from our teacher, or started Charley Stoddard reciting a poem, or set a girl singing. Before starting homeward, the whole party, including Shirley, shoes and stockings off, waded into the surf, and afterwards rested on the warm beds of sand. A fine comradeship, that, and one that never died.

Shirley, I should also mention, wrote some respectable poetry. I have fondly preserved, treasured, and cherished the original manuscript of a poem written by her at the time Margaret Fuller Ossoli was lost by shipwreck in 1850. This poem was included in my collection of California poetry, but was not printed in Outcroppings. I append it to this paper, of which it can hardly be considered an essential part.

I married and went to the mines, and our home was on the Mariposa Grant. We lived on a bed of gold. Once, upon a visit to the city, I found Shirley nervous and worn. Her vacation was about to begin. She went home with me, and stayed in bed the first three days. Then she was daily swung in a hammock under an oak. Soon we had horseback-rides, and up the creek she again panned out gold. Later we set out in the stage-coach for the hotel at the big Mariposa Grove. Mr. Lawrence put us in charge of Mr. Galen Clark, a rare scholar, and the guardian of the Big Tree Grove and of the Yosemite Valley. This charming man was much interested in Shirley. From the hotel we took daily rides with him through the great forest, and then made the twenty-five-mile horseback-ride and found Mr. James M. Hutchings, of the Illustrated California Magazine, awaiting us at the entrance to the valley. He escorted us to his picturesque hotel, where he and his interesting wife made our three weeks' stay most delightful. Down in the meadows we came upon John Muir sawing logs. He dropped his work, and we three went botanizing, and soon were learning all about the valley's formation as he entrancingly talked. We met many tourists of distinction, and Shirley forgot that she ever had a care, and on our way back she galloped along recklessly.

At our home in Mariposa we invited friends to come and enjoy Shirley's Shakespearean readings, chiefly comedy. In these Mr. Lawrence had a happy part.

In time Shirley went to New York, to her niece, Genevieve Stebbins, who was successful in a delightful line of art-work. Before leaving San Francisco, her faithful pupils and other friends gave a musicale and realized about two thousand dollars, which was presented her as a loving gift. In the great metropolis her genius was recognized soon after her arrival, and she was importuned to give lectures on art and literature. The Field family, who delightedly discovered her, took her to Europe, where she visited all the art-galleries, a treat that had been a lifelong heart's desire. In New York she had at once made her home with Dr. Ewer's widow and children, but, in the end, she went to Morristown, New Jersey, where, it was said, she again happily met and renewed her friendship with Bret Harte's accomplished and delightful wife and her attractive children, while Bret Harte himself was sojourning in Europe, a successful author. Mrs. John F. Swift, her long-time appreciative friend, Charley Stoddard, myself, and others, contributed to her pleasure by letters till the close of her perfect life at Morristown, New Jersey, on February 9, 1906. No other woman has left a more lasting impress on the California community. But back to Rich Bar! Back to the gold-fields! DAME SHIRLEY is abroad, and again she is weaving her wizard spell!

"ALONE"

A REMINISCENCE OF MARGARET FULLER OSSOLI

By Shirley Lee

Beneath thy spirit-eyes I stand alone,
    Nor deem thee of the dead
As mournfully I gaze, sad-hearted one,
    On that calm brow and head.

The starry crown of genius could not save
    From woman's gift of grief;
The moaning billows o'er thy breast that have
    Emblem thy life too brief.

O Margaret! my weak heart-pulses shiver
    In wordless woe for thee,
Thy wasted tenderness, thy love that never
    Might its fruition see.

Thou hadst no youth, O wondrous child! no youth
    Haloed thy later life;
Sternly thy girl heart sought its solemn truth
    In battle and in strife.

In thine own Northern home didst thou not live
    "Alone," always "alone"?
What heart to thine uplifted heart could give
    Ever an answering tone?

In suffering, labor, strife, we saw thee stand
    With lips that would not moan,
While shone thy regal brow and eyes with grand
    Aspirings all thine own.

At last among thy Romans thou didst find
    A shrine for that large heart;
It understood thee not, the Northern mind,
    But coldly shrunk apart,

When those pale lips—from whence, an hour agone,
    Flew out, like rifted light,
Winged words of wit—murmured their wailed "Alone"
    To the pitying midnight.

And I have read thy life, its mournful story
    Of loneliness and blight;
But o'er its close there shines a solemn glory,
    A setting star's trailed light.

Margaret! white-robed, thy hair unbound, thy veil,
    Most like a bride wert thou
When Ocean clasped thee, and, with lips all pale
    And icy, kissed thy brow.

And lovely as a white unfolded blossom
    Lay the child Angelo,
Hushed to his dreamless flower-sleep on that bosom
    Which would not let him go.

Husband, and wife, and child together flutter
    Up to the great white throne,
Where nevermore may Margaret Fuller utter
    That piteous "Alone!"

THE CONTENTS

THE JOURNEY TO RICH BAR

A thousand people and but one physician.
The author's husband seeks health and
business. Journey through deep snow, in
midsummer, to reach Rich Bar. The
revivifying effect of mountain atmosphere.
Arrival of twenty-nine physicians in less
than three weeks. The author's purpose to
leave San Francisco and join her husband at
the mines. Direful predictions and
disapprobation of friends. Indelicacy of her position among an almost
exclusively male population. Indians, ennui, cold. Leaves for
Marysville. Scanty fare on way. Meets husband. Falls from mule. An
exhausting ride. A midnight *petit souper* at Marysville. Dr. C. leaves
on muleback for Bidwell's Bar. The author follows in springless
wagon. Beautiful scenery. Marysville Buttes. Sierra Nevada. Indian
women, their near-nudity, beautiful limbs and lithe forms,
picturesqueness. Flower-seed gathering. Indian bread. Marvelous
handiwork of basketry. A dangerous precipice. A disclaimer of

bravery. Table Mountain. Arrival at Bidwell's Bar. Rejoins husband. Uninviting quarters. Proceed to Berry Creek.

THE JOURNEY TO RICH BAR

A moonlit midsummer-night's ride on muleback. Joyous beginning. The Indian trail lost. Camping out for the night. Attempts in morning to find the trail. A trying ride in the fierce heat of midday. The trail found. A digression of thirty miles. Lack of food, and seven more miles to ride. To rest impossible. Mad joy when within sight of Berry Creek Rancho. Congratulations upon escape from Indians on the trail. Frenchman and wife murdered. The journey resumed. Arrival at the "Wild Yankee's". A breakfast with fresh butter and cream. Indian bucks, squaws, and papooses. Their curiosity. Pride of an Indian on his ability to repeat one line of a song. Indian women. Extreme beauty of their limbs; slender ankles and statuesque feet; haggardness of expression and ugliness of features. Girl of sixteen, a "wildwood Cleopatra," an exception to the general hideousness. The California Indian not the Indian of the Leatherstocking tales. A stop at the Buckeye Rancho. Start for Pleasant Valley Rancho. The trail again lost. Camping out for the night. Growling bears. Arrive at Pleasant Valley Rancho. Flea-haunted shanty. Beauty of the wilderness. Quail and deer. The chaparrals, and their difficulty of penetration by the mules. Escape from a rattlesnake. Descending precipitous hill on muleback. Saddle-girth breaks. Harmless fall from the saddle. Triumphant entry into Rich Bar. Tribute to mulekind. The Empire Hotel. "A huge shingle palace."

RICH BAR—ITS HOTELS AND PIONEER FAMILIES

The Empire Hotel, *the* hotel of Rich Bar. The author safely ensconced therein. California might be called the "Hotel State," from the plenitude of its taverns, etc. The Empire the only two-story building in Rich Bar, and the only one there having glass windows. Built by gamblers for immoral purposes. The speculation a failure, its occupants being treated with contempt or pity. Building sold for a few hundred dollars. The new landlord of the Empire. The landlady, an example of the wear and tear of crossing the plains. Left behind her two children and an eight-months-old baby. Cooking for six people, her two-weeks-old baby kicking and screaming in champagne-basket cradle. "The sublime martyrdom of maternity". Left alone immediately after infant's birth. Husband dangerously ill, and cannot help. A kindly miner. Three other women at the Bar. The "Indiana girl". "Girl" a misnomer. "A gigantic piece of humanity". "Dainty" habits and herculean feats. A log-cabin family. Pretty and interesting children. "The Miners' Home". Its petite landlady tends bar. "Splendid material for social parties this winter."

LIFE AND FORTUNE AT THE BAR-DIGGINGS

Flashy shops and showy houses of San Francisco. Rich Bar charmingly fresh and original. A diminutive valley. Río de las Plumas, or Feather River. Rich Bar, the Barra Rica of the Spaniards. An acknowledgment of "a most humiliating consciousness of geological deficiencies". Palatial splendor of the Empire Hotel. Round tents, square tents, plank hovels, log cabins, etc. "Local habitations" formed of pine boughs, and covered with old calico shirts. The "office" of Dr. C. excites the risibilities of the author. One of the "finders" of Rich Bar. Had not spoken to a woman for two years. Honors the occasion by an "investment" in champagne. The author assists in drinking to the honor of her arrival at the Bar. Nothing done in California without the sanctifying influence of the "spirit". History of the discovery of gold at Rich Bar. Thirty-three pounds of gold in eight hours. Fifteen hundred dollars from a panful of "dirt". Five hundred miners arrive at Rich Bar in about a week. Smith Bar, Indian Bar, Missouri Bar, and other bars. Miners extremely fortunate. Absolute wealth in a few weeks. Drunken gamblers in less than a year. Suffering for necessaries of life. A mild winter. A stormy spring. Impassable trails. No pack-mule trains arrive. Miners pack flour on their backs for over forty miles. Flour sells at over three dollars a pound. Subsistence on feed-barley. A voracious miner. An abundance placed in storage.

ACCIDENTS—SURGERY—DEATH—FESTIVITY

Frightful accidents to which the gold-seeker is constantly liable. Futile attempts of physician to save crushed leg of young miner. Universal outcry against amputation. Dr. C, however, uses the knife. Professional reputation at stake. Success attends the operation. Death of another young miner, who fell into mining-shaft. His funeral. Picturesque appearance of the miners thereat. Of what the miner's costume consists. Horror of the author aroused in contemplation of the lonely mountain-top graveyard. Jostling of life and death. Celebration of the anniversary of Chilian independence. Participation of a certain class of Yankees therein. The procession. A Falstaffian leader. The feast. A twenty-gallon keg of brandy on the table, gracefully encircled by quart dippers. The Chileños reel with a better grace, the Americans more naturally.

DEATH OF A MOTHER—LIFE OF PIONEER WOMEN

Death of one of the four pioneer women of Rich Bar. The funeral from the log-cabin residence. Sickly ten-months-old baby moans piteously for its mother. A handsome girl of six years, unconscious of her bereavement, shocks the author by her actions. A monte-table cover as a funeral pall. Painful feelings when nails are driven into coffin. The extempore prayer. Every observance possible surrounded the funeral. Visit to a canvas house of three "apartments". Barroom, dining-room, kitchen with bed-closet. A sixty-eight-pound woman. "A magnificent woman, a wife of the right sort". "Earnt her 'old man' nine hundred dollars in nine weeks, by washing". The "manglers" and the "mangled". Fortitude of refined California women pioneers. The orphaned girl a "cold-blooded little wretch". Remorse of the author. "Baby decanters". The gayety and fearlessness of the orphaned girl.

USE OF PROFANITY—UNCERTAINTY OF MINING

Prevalence of profanity in California. Excuses for its use. A mere slip of the tongue, etc. Grotesqueness of some blasphemous expressions. Sleep-killing mining machinery. What a flume is. Project to flume the river for many miles. The California mining system a gambling or lottery transaction. Miner who works his own claim the more successful. Dr. C. a loser in his mining ventures. Another sleep-killer. Bowling-alleys. Bizarre cant phrases and slang used by the miners. "Honest Indian?" "Talk enough when horses fight". "Talk enough between gentlemen". "I've got the dead-wood on him". "I'm going nary cent" (on person mistrusted). All carry the freshness of originality to the ear of the author.

THE NEW LOG-CABIN HOME AT INDIAN BAR

Change of residence to Indian Bar. Whether to go to the new camp on muleback over the hill, or on foot by crossing the river. The water-passage decided upon. An escort of Indian Barians. Magnificence of scenery on the way. Gold-miners at work. Their implements. "The color". The Stars and Stripes on a lofty treetop. A camp of tents and cabins. Some of calico shirts and pine boughs. Indian Bar described. Mountains shut out the sun. The "Humbolt" (spelled without the *d* on the sign) the only hotel in the camp. A barroom with a dancing-floor. A cook who plays the violin. A popular place. Clinking glasses and swaggering drinkers. "No place for a lady". The log-cabin residence. Its primitive, makeshift furnishings. The library. No churches, society, etc. "No vegetables but potatoes and onions, no milk, no eggs, no *nothing*."

LIFE AND CHARACTERS AT INDIAN BAR

THEFT OF GOLD-DUST—TRIAL AND PUNISHMENT

and smart". The "Indiana girl" impossible to Yank. "A superior and splendid woman, but no polish". Yank's "olla podrida of heterogeneous merchandise". The author meets the banished gold-dust thief. Subscription by the miners on his banishment. A fool's errand to establish his innocence. An oyster-supper bet. The thief's statements totally incompatible with innocence.

AMATEUR MINING—HAIRBREADTH 'SCAPES, &C.

Three dollars and twenty-five cents in gold-dust. Sorry she learned the trade. The resulting losses and suffering. Secret of the brilliant successes of former gold-washeresses. Salting the ground by miners in order to deceive their fair visitors. Erroneous ideas of the richness of auriferous dirt resulting therefrom. Rarity of lucky strikes. Claim yielding ten dollars a day considered valuable. Consternation and near-disaster in the author's cabin. Trunk of forest giant rolls down hill. Force broken by rock near cabin. Terror of careless woodman. Another narrow escape at Smith's Bar. Pursuit and escape of woodman. Two sudden deaths at Indian Bar. Inquest in the open. Cosmopolitan gathering thereat. Wife of one of the deceased an advanced bloomer. Animadversions on strong-minded bloomers seeking their rights. California pheasant, the gallina del campo of the Spaniards. Pines and dies in captivity. Smart, harmless earthquake-shocks.

ROBBERY, TRIAL, EXECUTION—MORE TRAGEDY

Theft of gold-dust. Arrest of two suspected miners. Trial and acquittal at miners' meeting. Robbed persons still believe the accused guilty. Suspects leave mountains. One returns, and plan for his detection proves successful. Confronted with evidence of guilt, discloses, on promise of immunity from prosecution, hiding-place of gold-dust. Miners, however, try him, and on conviction he is sentenced to be hanged one hour thereafter. Miners' mode of trial. Respite of three hours. Bungling execution. Drunken miner's proposal for sign of guilt or innocence. Corpse "enwrapped in white shroud of feathery snowflakes". Execution the work of the more reckless. Not generally approved. The Squire, disregarded, protested. Miners' procedure compared with the moderation of the first Vigilance Committee of San Francisco. Singular disappearance of body of miner. Returning to the States with his savings, his two companions report their leaving him in dying condition. Arrest and fruitless investigation. An unlikely bequest of money. Trial and acquittal of the miner's companions. Their story improbable, their actions like actual murder.

A STORMY WINTER—HOLIDAY SATURNALIAS

Saturnalia in camp. Temptations of riches. Tribute to the miners. Dreariness of camp-life during stormy winter weather. Christmas and change of proprietors at the Humboldt. Preparations for a double celebration. Muleback loads of brandy-casks and champagne-baskets. Noisy procession of revelers. Oyster-and-champagne supper. Three days of revelry. Trial by mock vigilance committee. Judgment to "treat the crowd". Revels resumed on larger scale at New Year's. Boat-loads of drunken miners fall into river. Saved by being drunk. Boat-load of bread falls into river and floats down-stream. Pulley-and-rope device for hauling boat across river. Fiddlers "nearly fiddled themselves into the grave". Liquors "beginning to look scarce". Subdued and sheepish-looking bacchanals. Nothing extenuated, nor aught set down in malice. Boating on river. Aquatic plants. Bridge swept away in torrent. Loss of canoe. Branch from moss-grown fir-tree "a cornice wreathed with purple-starred tapestry". A New Year's present from the river. A two-inch spotted trout. No fresh meat for a month. "Dark and ominous rumors". Dark hams, rusty pork, etc., stored.

SOCIABILITY AND EXCITEMENTS OF MINING-LIFE

Departure from Indian Bar of the mulatto Ned. His birthday-celebration dinner, at which the New Year's piscatory phenomenon figures in the bill of fare. A total disregard of dry laws at the dinner. Excitement over reported discovery of quartz-mines. A complete humbug. Charges of salting. Excitement renewed upon report of other new quartz-mines. Even if rich, lack of proper machinery would render the working thereof impossible. Prediction that quartz-mining eventually will be the most profitable. Miners leave the river without paying their debts. Pursued and captured. Miners' court orders settlement in full. Celebration, by French miners on the river, of the Revolution of 1848. Invitation to dine at best-built log cabin on the river. The habitation of five or six young miners. A perfect marvel of a fireplace. Huge unsplit logs as firewood. Window of glass jars. Possibilities in the use of empty glass containers. Unthrift of some miners. The cabin, its furniture, store of staple provisions, chinaware, cutlery. The dinner in the cabin. A cow kept. Wonderful variety of makeshift candlesticks in use among the miners. Dearth of butter, potatoes, onions, fresh meat, in camp. Indian-summer weather at Indian Bar. A cozy retreat in the hills. A present of feathered denizens of the mountains. Roasted for dinner.

SPRINGTIDE—LINGUISTICS—STORMS—ACCIDENTS

The splendor of a March morning in the mountains of California. The first bird of the season. Blue and red shirted miners a feature of the landscape. "Wanderers from the whole broad earth". The languages of many nations heard. How the Americans attempt to converse with the Spanish-speaking population. "Sabe," "vamos," "poco tiempo," "si," and "bueno," a complete lexicon of la lengua castellana, in the minds of the Americans. An "ugly disposition" manifested when the speaker is not understood. The Spaniards "ain't kinder like our folks," nor "folksy". Mistakes not all on one side. Spanish proverb regarding certain languages. Not complimentary to English. Stormy weather. Storm king a perfect Proteus. River on a rampage. Sawmill carried away. Pastimes of the miners during the storm. MS. account of storm sent in keg via river to Marysville newspaper. Silversmith makes gold rings during storm. Raffling and reraffling of same as pastime. Some natural gold rings. Nugget in shape of eagle's head presented to author. Miners buried up to neck in cave-in. Escape with but slight injury. Miner stabbed without provocation in drunken frolic. Life despaired of at first. No notice taken of affair.

MINING METHODS—MINERS, GAMBLERS, &C.

Difficulty experienced in writing amid the charms of California mountain scenery. Science the blindest guide on a gold-hunting expedition. Irreverent contempt of the beautiful mineral to the dictates of science. Nothing better to be expected from the root of all evil. Foreigners more successful than Americans in its pursuit. Americans always longing for big strikes. Success lies in staying and persevering. How a camp springs into existence. Prospecting, panning out, and discovery that it pays. The claim. Building the shanty. Spreading of news of the new diggings. Arrival of the monte-dealers. Industrious begin digging for gold. The claiming system. How claims worked. Working difficult amidst huge mountain rocks. Partnerships then compulsory. Naming the mine or company. The long-tom. Panning out the gold. Sinking shaft to reach bed-rock. Drifting coyote-holes in search of crevices. Water-ditches and water companies. Washing out in long-tom. Waste-ditches. Tailings. Fluming companies. Rockers. Gold-mining is nature's great lottery scheme. Thousands taken out in a few hours. Six ounces in six months. "Almost all seem to have lost". Jumped claims. Caving in of excavations. Abandonment of expensive paying shafts. Miner making "big strike" almost sure prey of professional gamblers. As spring opens, gamblers flock in like birds of prey. After stay of only four days, gambler leaves Bar with over a thousand dollars of miners' gold. As many foreigners as Americans on the river. Foreigners generally extremely ignorant and degraded. Some Spaniards of the highest education and accomplishment. Majority of Americans mechanics of better class. Sailors and farmers next in number. A few merchants and steamboat-clerks. A few physicians. One lawyer. Ranchero of distinguished appearance an accomplished monte-dealer and horse-jockey. Is said to have been a preacher in the States. Such not uncommon for California.

BIRTH—STABBING—FOREIGNERS OUSTED—REVELS

California mountain flora. A youthful Kanaka mother. Her feat of pedestrianism. Stabbing of a Spaniard by an American. The result of a request to pay a debt. Nothing done and but little said about the atrocity. Foreigners barred from working at Rich Bar. Spaniards thereupon move to Indian Bar. They erect places for the sale of intoxicants. Many new houses for public entertainment at Indian Bar. Sunday "swearing, drinking, gambling, and fighting". Salubrity of the climate. No death for months, except by accidental drowning in flood-water. Capture of two grizzly cubs. "The oddest possible pets". "An echo from the outside world once a month."

SUPPLIES BY PACK-MULES—KANAKAS AND INDIANS

Belated arrival of pack-mule train with much-needed supplies. Picturesque appearance of the dainty-footed mules descending the steep hills. Of every possible color. Gay trappings. Tinkling bells. Peculiar urging cry of the Spanish muleteers. Lavish expenditure of gold-dust for vegetables and butter. Potatoes forty cents a pound. Incense of the pungent member of the lily family. Arrival of other storm-bound trains, and sudden collapse in prices. A horseback-ride on dangerous mule-trail. Fall of oxen over precipice. The mountain flowers, oaks, and rivulets. Visit to Kanaka mother. A beauty from the isles. Hawaiian superstition. An unfortunate request for the baby as a present. Consolatory promise to give the next one. Indian visitors. Head-dresses. "Very tight and very short shirts". Indian mode of life. Their huts, food, cooking, utensils, manner of eating. Sabine-like invasion leaves to tribe but a few old squaws. "Startlingly unsophisticated state of almost entire nudity". Their filthy habits. Papooses fastened in framework of light wood. Indian modes of fishing. A handsome but shy young buck. Classic gracefulness of folds of white-sheet robe of Indian. Light and airy step of the Indians something superhuman. Miserably brutish and degraded. Their vocabulary of about twenty words. Their love of gambling, and its frightful consequences. Arrival of hundreds of people at Indian Bar. Saloons springing up in every direction. Fluming operations rapidly progressing. A busy, prosperous summer looked for.

FOURTH OF JULY FESTIVAL—SPANISH ATTACKED

Fourth of July celebration at Rich Bar. The author makes the flag. Its materials. How California was represented therein. Floated from the top of a lofty pine-tree. The decorations at the Empire Hotel. An "officious Goth" mars the floral piece designed for the orator of the day. Only two ladies in the audience. Two others are expected, but do not arrive. No copy of the Declaration of Independence. Some preliminary speeches by political aspirants. Orator of the day reads anonymous poem. Oration "exceedingly fresh and new". Belated arrival of the expected ladies, new-comers from the East. With new fashions, they extinguish the author and her companion. Dinner at the Empire. Mexican War captain as president. "Toasts quite spicy and original". Fight in the barroom. Eastern lady "chose to go faint" at sight of blood. Cabin full of "infant phenomena". A rarity in the mountains. Miners, on way home from celebration, give nine cheers for mother and children. Outcry at Indian Bar against Spaniards. Several severely wounded. Whisky and patriotism. Prejudices and arrogant assurance accounted for. Misinterpretation by the foreigner. Injustices by the lower classes against Spaniards pass unnoticed. Innumerable drunken fights. Broken heads and collarbones, stabbings. "Sabbaths almost always enlivened by such merry events". Body of Frenchman found in river. Murder evident. Suspicion falls on nobody.

MURDER, THEFT, RIOT, HANGING, WHIPPING, &C.

Three weeks of excitement at Indian Bar. Murders, fearful accidents, bloody deaths, whippings, hanging, an attempted suicide, etc. Sabbath-morning walk in the hills. Miners' ditch rivaling in beauty the work of nature. Fatal stabbing by a Spaniard. He afterwards parades street with a Mexicana, brandishing along bloody knife. His pursuit by and escape from the infuriated Americans. Unfounded rumor of conspiracy of the Spaniards to murder the Americans. Spaniards barricade themselves. Grief of Spanish woman over corpse of murdered man. Miners arrive from Rich Bar. Wild cry for vengeance, and for expulsion of Spaniards. The author prevailed upon to retire to place of safety. Accidental discharge of gun when drunken owner of vile resort attempts to force way through armed guard. Two seriously wounded. Sobering effect of the accident. Vigilance committee organized. Suspected Spaniards arrested. Trial of the Mexicana. Always wore male attire, was foremost in fray, and, armed with brace of pistols, fought like a fury. Sentenced to leave by daylight. Indirect cause of fight. Woman always to blame. Trial of ringleaders. Sentences of whipping, and to leave. Confiscation of property for benefit of wounded. Anguish of the author when Spaniards were whipped. Young Spaniard movingly but vainly pleads for death instead of whipping. His oath to murder every American he should afterwards meet alone. Doubtless will keep his word. Murder of Mr. Bacon, a ranchero, for his money, by his negro cook. Murderer caught at Sacramento with part of money. His trial at Rich Bar by the vigilantes. Sentence of death by hanging. Another negro attempts suicide. Accuses the mulatto Ned of attempt to murder him. Dr. C. in trouble for binding up negro's self-inflicted wounds. Formation of "Moguls," who make night hideous. Vigilantes do not interfere. Duel at Missouri Bar. Fatal results. A large crowd present. Vigilance committee also present. "But you must remember that this is California."

MURDER—MINING SCENES—SPANISH BREAKFAST

Ramada, unoccupied, wrecked by log rolling down hill. Was place of residence of wounded Spaniard, who had died but a few days previously. Murder near Indian Bar. Innocent and harmless person arrested, said to answer description of murderer. A humorous situation. A "guard of honor" from the vigilantes while in custody. Upon release his expenses all paid. Enjoyed a holiday from hard work. Tendered a present and a handsome apology. Public opinion in the mines a cruel but fortunately a fickle thing. Invitation to author to breakfast at Spanish garden. The journey thereto, along river, with its busy mining scenes. The wing-dam, and how it differs from the ordinary dam. An involuntary bath. Drifts, shafts, coyote-holes. How claims are worked. Flumes. Unskilled workmen. Their former professions or occupations. The best water in California, but the author is unappreciative. Flavorless, but, since the Flood, always tastes of sinners. Don Juan's country-seat. The Spanish breakfast. The eatables and the drinkables. Stronger spirits for the stronger spirits. Ice, through oversight, the only thing lacking. Yank's tame cub. Parodic doggerel by the author on her loss of pets. A miners' dinner-party with but one teaspoon, and that one borrowed. An unlearned and wearisome blacksmith.

DISCOMFORTS OF TRIP TO POLITICAL CONVENTION

Visit to the American Valley. Journey thither. Scenes by the way. Political convention. Delegates from Indian Bar. Arrival at Greenwood's Rancho, headquarters of Democrats. Overcrowded. Party proceed to the American Rancho, headquarters of Whigs. Also overcrowded. Tiresome ride of ladies on horseback. Proceed to house of friend of lady in party. An inhospitable reception. The author entertains herself. Men of party return to the American Rancho. Fearful inroad upon the eatables. Landlord aghast, but pacified by generous orders for drinkables. California houses not proof against eavesdroppers. Misunderstandings and explanations overheard by the author. Illness of hostess. Uncomfortable and miserable night, and worse quarters. Handsome riding-habit, etc., of the hostess. Table-service, carpeting, chests of tea, casks of sugar, bags of coffee, etc., "the good people possessed everything but a house". "The most beautiful spot I ever saw in California". Owner building house of huge hewn logs. The author returns to the American Rancho. Its primitive furniture, etc. Political visitors. The convention. Horse-racing and gambling. The author goes to Greenwood's Rancho. More primitive furniture and lack of accommodations. Misplaced benevolence of Bostonians. Should transfer their activities to California.

THE OVERLAND TIDE OF IMMIGRATION

Exoneration of landlords for conditions at Greenwood's Rancho. The American Valley. Prospective summer resort. Prodigious vegetables. New England scenery compared with that of California. Greenwood's Rancho. Place of origin of quartz hoax. Beautiful stones. Recruiting-place of overland immigrants. Haggard immigrant women. Death and speedy burial on the plains. Handsome young widow immigrant. Aspirants to matrimony candidates for her hand. Interesting stories of adventures on the plains. Four women, sisters or sisters-in-law, and their thirty-six children. Accomplished men. Infant prodigies. A widow with eight sons and one daughter. Primitive laundering, but generous patrons. The bloomer costume appropriate for overland journey. Dances in barroom. Unwilling female partners. Some illiterate immigrants. Many intelligent and well-bred women. The journey back to Indian Bar. The tame frog in the rancho barroom. The dining-table a bed at night. Elation of the author on arriving at her own log cabin.

MINING FAILURES—DEPARTURE FROM INDIAN BAR

Dread of spending another winter at Indian Bar. Failure of nearly all the fluming companies. Official report of one company. Incidental failure of business people. The author's preparations to depart. Prediction of early rains. High prices cause of dealers' failure to lay in supply of provisions. Probable fatal results to families unable to leave Bar. Rain and snow alternately. The Squire a poor weather prophet. Pack-mule trains with provisions fail to arrive. Amusement found in petty litigation. Legal acumen of the Squire. He wins golden opinions. The judgment all the prevailing party gets. What the constable got in effort to collect judgment. Why Dr. C.'s fee was not paid. A prescription of "calumny and other pizen doctor's stuff". A wonderful gold specimen in the form of a basket. "Weighs about two dollars and a half". How little it takes to make people comfortable. A log-cabin meal and its table-service. The author departs on horseback from Indian Bar. Her regrets upon leaving the mountains. "Feeble, half-dying invalid not recognizable in your now perfectly healthy sister."

THE ILLUSTRATIONS

1. Gold-washing in Wicker Baskets—Americans and Hispano-Californians with Indians

This is a composite engraving, a very interesting feature of which is the Indians and their wicker baskets, the latter going out of use when metal pans were obtainable, which also displaced wooden bowls and homely makeshifts. This feature is resketched from a rare old print in the possession of the Van Ness family of San Francisco. The huts are specimens of ramadas, popular with the Spanish-speaking miners, and frequently mentioned by Shirley.

2. Sutter's Mill, Coloma, where Gold was Accidentally Discovered in January, 1848

This fine engraving follows closely, in all essential details, that in the Voyages en Californie et dans l'Orégon, par M. de Saint-Amant, Envoyé du Gouvernement Français, en 1851-1852 (Paris, 1854). The engravings in that volume, although poorly printed on a cheap grade of book-paper, are noted for their accuracy, and are interesting as showing the methods etc. of the miners while Shirley was writing her Letters. The tail-race, in the foreground, is where James Wilson Marshall and Peter L. Wimmer first saw the nuggets, but Marshall was the first to pick up a specimen. Much has been written of Marshall; the Wimmers were of the Western pioneer type.

3. Ground-sluicing

This spirited engraving is resketched, in essentials, from a woodcut in Henry De Groot's Recollections of California Mining Life (1884), also in his Gold Mines and Mining in

California (1885). Ground-sluicing is done in winter, when water is abundant and the ground soft, the pay-dirt being thrown into a channel made for the purpose, and down which the water rushes. The gold settles on the bed-rock, and is collected later, when the water-run has subsided.

4. Pan, Cradle or Rocker, Long-tom, Sluice-washing—Drifting, Windlass and Shaft

The varied and animated scene depicted in this plate is resketched from De Groot's Gold Mines and Mining in California. (See note to plate 3.) In the foreground, on the left, a miner washes dirt in a pan. Above, and to the left, a miner washes in a rocker or cradle, the pay-dirt coming in a tram-car from the tunnel, in which are drift-diggings. The men at the windlass are sinking a shaft, prospecting for drift-deposits. To the right, in the foreground, three men are working a long-tom, which, in point of time, followed the rocker. One of the miners is keeping the dirt stirred up in the tom, under which is set a riffle-box with quicksilver to catch the gold. In the background miners are hand or shovel sluicing, in which the riffle-box of the long-tom is dispensed with.

5. Interior of Miners' Log Cabin—One Partner Cooking for Night-faring Visitors

This interesting engraving also follows, in all essentials, that in de Saint-Amant's Voyages. (See note to plate 2, supra.) The owners of the cabin had evidently retired for the night, and were awakened by their visitors. The upper bunk, or berth, has been vacated by the miner cooking. We will say two of the visitors have been prospecting, and are reasoning with the third, who appears to have come from that state of the Union "where one must demonstrate." The rifle close to the bunk of the sleeping miner, the mining implements littered over the floor, the bottles etc. on the shelf-table, are features that require no explanation.

6. Saloon in a Mining-camp—Monte-dealer, Miners, Española and Mexicana

This is a composite engraving, the artist having combined several old prints. The Spanish woman is shown in a national costume, and her air and attitude indicate her ability to take care of herself. The Mexican girl at the bar, and armed, is a type of the Mexicana mentioned by Shirley.

7. Washing in Rockers on River's Brink—Miners Packing Pay-gravel in Buckets

This realistic plate follows closely, in essentials, that in de Saint-Amant's Voyages. (See note to plate 2, ante.) The bare declivity has evidently been worked, and the auriferous gravel must now be packed from the heights. A barrow with shafts at only one end may be seen beside one of the rockers, and it is conjectured that not all the gravel is picked in buckets. The miner seen in the background of brushwood digs the pay-gravel.

8. Washing in Long-tom with Water from Flume—Cheaper than Pumping from River

This beautiful engraving follows closely that in de Saint-Amant's Voyages. (See note to plate 2, ante.) Here the miners found it more economical to purchase water from a fluming company than to pump it from the river. The belt and pulley is used to drive a Chinese pump which keeps dry the pit now being worked.

The Shirley Letters

Letter the First

Part One

The Journey to Rich Bar

Rich Bar, East Branch of the North Fork of Feather River,

September 13, 1851.

 I can easily imagine, dear M., the look of large wonder which gleams from your astonished eyes when they fall upon the date of this letter. I can figure to myself your whole surprised attitude as you exclaim, "What, in the name of all that is restless, has sent 'Dame Shirley' to Rich Bar? How did such a shivering, frail, home-loving little thistle ever float safely to that far-away spot, and take root so kindly, as it evidently has, in that barbarous soil? Where, in this living, breathing world of ours, lieth that same Rich Bar, which, sooth to say, hath a most taking name? And, for pity's sake, how does the poor little fool expect to amuse herself there?"

Patience, sister of mine. Your curiosity is truly laudable, and I trust that before you read the postscript of this epistle it will be fully and completely relieved. And, first, I will merely observe, *en passant*, reserving a full description of its discovery for a future letter, that said Bar forms a part of a mining settlement situated on the East Branch of the North Fork of Feather River, "away off up in the mountains," as our "little Faresoul" would say, at almost the highest point where, as yet, gold has been discovered, and indeed within fifty miles of the summit of the Sierra Nevada itself. So much, at present, for our *local*, while I proceed to tell you of the propitious—or unpropitious, as the result will prove—winds which blew us hitherward.

You already know that F., after suffering for an entire year with fever and ague, and bilious, remittent, and intermittent fevers,—this delightful list varied by an occasional attack of jaundice,—was advised, as a *dernier ressort*, to go into the mountains. A friend, who had just returned from the place, suggested Rich Bar as the terminus of his health-seeking journey, not only on account of the extreme purity of the atmosphere, but because there were more than a thousand people there already, and but one physician, and as his strength increased, he might find in that vicinity a favorable opening for the practice of his profession, which, as the health of his purse was almost as feeble as that of his body, was not a bad idea.

F. was just recovering from a brain-fever when he concluded to go to the mines; but, in spite of his excessive debility, which rendered him liable to chills at any hour of the day or night, he started on the seventh day of June—mounted on a mule, and accompanied by a jackass to carry his baggage, and a friend who kindly volunteered to assist him in spending his money—for this wildly beautiful spot. F. was compelled by sickness to stop several days on the road. He suffered intensely, the trail for many miles being covered to the depth of twelve feet with snow, although it was almost midsummer when he passed over it. He arrived at Rich Bar the latter part of June, and found the revivifying effect of its bracing atmosphere far surpassing his most sanguine hopes. He soon built himself an office, which was a perfect marvel to the miners, from its superior elegance. It is the only one on the Bar, and I intend to visit it in a day or two, when I will give you a description of its architectural splendors. It will perhaps enlighten you as to one peculiarity of a newly discovered mining district, when I inform you that although there were but two or three physicians at Rich Bar when my husband arrived, in less than three weeks there were *twenty-nine* who had chosen this place for the express purpose of practicing their profession.

Finding his health so almost miraculously improved, F. concluded, should I approve the plan, to spend the winter in the mountains. I had teased him to let me accompany him when he left in June, but he had at that time refused, not daring to subject me to inconveniences, of the extent of which he was himself ignorant. When the letter disclosing his plans for the winter reached me at San Francisco, I was perfectly enchanted. You know that I am a regular nomad in my passion for wandering. Of course my numerous acquaintances in San Francisco raised one universal shout of disapprobation. Some said that I ought to be put into a straitjacket, for I was undoubtedly mad to think of such a thing. Some said that I should never get there alive, and if I *did*, would not stay a month; that it was ever my lot to be victimized in, and commenced my journey in earnest. I was the only passenger. For thirty miles the road passed through as beautiful a country as I had ever seen. Dotted here and there with the California oak, it reminded me of the peaceful apple-orchards and smiling river-meadows of dear old New England. As a frame to the graceful picture, on one side rose the Buttes, that group of hills so piquant and saucy, and on the other, tossing to heaven the everlasting whiteness of their snow-wreathed foreheads, stood, sublime in their very monotony, the summits of the glorious Sierra Nevada.

We passed one place where a number of Indian women were gathering flower-seeds, which, mixed with pounded acorns and grasshoppers, form the bread of these miserable people. The idea, and the really ingenious mode of carrying it out, struck me as so singular, that I cannot forbear attempting a description. These poor creatures were entirely naked, with the exception of a quantity of grass bound round the waist, and covering the thighs midway to the knees, perhaps. Each one carried two brown baskets, which, I have since been told, are made of a species of osier, woven with a neatness which is absolutely marvelous, when one considers that they are the handiwork of such degraded wretches. Shaped like a cone, they are about six feet in circumference at the opening, and I should judge them to be nearly three feet in depth. It is evident, by the grace and care with which they handle them, that they are exceedingly light. It is possible that my description may be inaccurate, for I have never read any account of them, and merely give my own impressions as they were received while the wagon rolled rapidly by the spot at which the women were at work. One of these queer baskets is suspended from the back, and is kept in place by a thong of leather passing across the forehead. The other they carry in the right hand and wave over the flower-seeds, first to the right, and back again to the left, alternately, as they walk slowly along, with a motion as regular and monotonous as that of a mower. When they have collected a handful of the seeds, they pour them into the basket behind, and continue this work until they have filled the latter with their strange harvest. The seeds thus gathered are carried to their rancherías, and stowed away with great care for winter use. It was, to me, very interesting to watch their regular motion, they seemed so exactly to keep time with one another; and with their dark shining skins, beautiful limbs, and lithe forms, they were by no means the least picturesque feature of the landscape.

Ten miles this side of Bidwell's Bar, the road, hitherto so smooth and level, became stony and hilly. For more than a mile we drove along the edge of a precipice, and so near, that it seemed to me, should the horses deviate a hairbreadth from their usual track, we must be dashed into eternity. Wonderful to relate, I did not "Oh!" nor "Ah!" nor shriek *once*, but remained crouched in the back of the wagon, as silent as death. When we were again in safety, the driver exclaimed, in the classic patois of New England, "Wall, I guess yer the fust woman that ever rode over that are hill without hollering." He evidently did not know that it was the intensity of my *fear* that kept me so still.

Soon Table Mountain became visible, extended like an immense dining-board for the giants, its summit a perfectly straight line penciled for more than a league against the glowing sky. And now we found ourselves among the Red Hills, which look like an ascending sea of crimson waves, each crest foaming higher and higher as we creep among them, until we drop down suddenly into the pretty little valley called Bidwell's Bar.

I arrived there at three o'clock in the evening, when I found F. in much better health than when he left Marysville. As there was nothing to sleep *in* but a tent, and nothing to sleep *on* but the ground, and the air was black with the fleas hopping about in every direction, we concluded to ride forward to the Berry Creek House, a ranch ten miles farther on our way, where we proposed to pass the night.

Letter the First

Part Two

[The Pioneer, February, 1854]

The JOURNEY to RICH BAR

SYNOPSIS

A moonlit midsummer-night's ride on muleback. Joyous beginning. The Indian trail lost. Camping out for the night- Attempts in the morning to find the trail. A trying ride in the fierce heat of midday. The trail found. A digression of thirty miles. Lack of food, and seven miles more to ride. To rest is impossible. Mad joy when within sight of Berry Creek Rancho. Congratulations on escape from Indians on trail. Frenchman and wife murdered. The journey resumed. Arrival at the "Wild Yankee's". Breakfast with fresh butter and cream. Indian bucks, squaws, and papooses. Their curiosity. Pride of an Indian in ability to repeat one line of a song. Indian women: extreme beauty of their limbs; slender ankles and statuesque feet; haggardness of expression and ugliness of features. Girl of sixteen, a "wildwood Cleopatra," an exception to the general hideousness. The California Indian not the Indian of the Leatherstocking tales. A stop at the Buckeye Rancho. Start for Pleasant Valley Rancho. The trail again lost. Camping out for the night. Growling bears. Arrive at Pleasant Valley Rancho. A flea-haunted shanty. The beauty of the wilderness. Quail and deer. The chaparrals, and their difficulty of penetration by the mules. Escape from a rattlesnake. Descending precipitous hill on muleback.

Saddle-girth breaks. Harmless fall from the saddle. Triumphant entry into Rich Bar. A tribute to mulekind. The Empire Hotel. "A huge shingle palace."

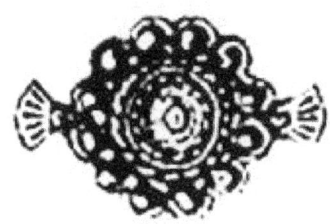

Letter the First

Part Two

The Journey to Rich Bar

Rich Bar, East Branch of the North Fork of Feather River,

September 13, 1851.

 The moon was just rising as we started. The air made one think of fairy-festivals, of living in the woods *always*, with the green-coated people for playmates, it was so wonderfully soft and cool, without the least particle of dampness. A midsummer's night in the leafy month of June, amid the dreamiest haunts of "Old Crownest," could not be more enchantingly lovely.

We sped merrily onward until nine o'clock, making the old woods echo with song and story and laughter, for F. was unusually gay, and I was in tip-top spirits. It seemed to me so *funny* that we two people should be riding on mules, all by ourselves, in these glorious latitudes, night smiling down so kindly upon us, and, funniest of *all*, that we were going to live in the Mines! In spite of my gayety, however, I now began to wonder why we did not arrive at our intended lodgings. F. reassured me by saying that when we had *de*scended this hill or *as*cended that, we should certainly be there. But ten o'clock came; eleven, twelve, one, *two*! but no Berry Creek House! I began to be frightened, and besides that, was very sick with a nervous headache. At every step we were getting higher and higher into the mountains, and even F. was at last compelled to acknowledge that we were *lost*! We were on an Indian trail, and the bushes grew so low that at almost every step I was obliged to bend my forehead to my mule's neck. This increased the pain in my head to an almost insupportable degree. At last I told F. that I could not remain in the saddle a moment longer. Of course there was nothing to do but to camp. Totally unprepared for such a catastrophe, we had nothing but the blankets of our mules, and a thin quilt in which I had rolled some articles necessary for the journey, because it was easier to pack than a traveling-bag. F. told me to sit on the mule while he prepared my woodland couch, but I was too nervous for that, and so jumped off and dropped onto the ground, worn out with fatigue and pain. The night was still dreamily beautiful, and I should have been enchanted with the adventure (for I had fretted and complained a good deal, because we had no *excuse* for camping out) had it not been for that impertinent headache, which, you remember, always *would* visit me at the most inconvenient seasons.

About daylight, somewhat refreshed, we again mounted our mules, confidently believing that an hour's ride would bring us to the Berry Creek House, as we supposed, of course, that we had camped in its immediate vicinity. We tried more than a dozen paths, which, as they led *nowhere*, we would retrace to the principal trail. At last F. determined to keep upon one, as it *must*, he thought, in *time*, lead us out of the mountains, even if we landed on the other side of California. Well, we rode on, and on, and on, up hill and down hill, down hill and up, through fir-groves and oak-clumps, and along the edge of dark ravines, until I thought that I should go *mad*, for all this time the sun was pouring down its hottest rays most pitilessly, and I had an excruciating pain in my head and in all my limbs.

About two o'clock we struck the main trail, and, meeting a man,—the first human being that we had seen since we left Bidwell's,—were told that we were seven miles from the Berry Creek House, and that we had been down to the North Fork of the American River, more than thirty miles out of our way! This joyful news gave us fresh strength, and we rode on as fast as our worn-out mules could go.

Although we had eaten nothing since noon the day before, I bore up bravely until we arrived within two miles of the rancho, when courage and strength both gave way, and I *implored* F. to let me lie down under a tree and rest for a few hours. He very wisely refused, knowing that if I dismounted it would be impossible to get me onto my mule again, and we should be obliged to spend another night under the stars, which, in this enchanting climate, would have been delightful, had we possessed any food; but, knowing that I needed refreshment even more than I did rest, he was compelled to insist upon my proceeding.

My poor husband! He must have had a trying time with me, for I sobbed and cried like the veriest child, and repeatedly declared that I should never live to get to the rancho. F. said afterwards that he began to think I intended to keep my word, for I certainly *looked* like a dying person.

O Mary! it makes me *shudder* when I think of the mad joy with which I saw that rancho! Remember that, with the exception of three or four hours the night before, we had been in the saddle for nearly twenty-four hours without refreshment. When we stopped, F. carried me into the house and laid me onto a bunk, though I have no remembrance of it, and he said that when he offered me some food, I turned from it with disgust, exclaiming, "Oh, take it away! give me some cold water and let me *sleep*, and be sure you don't wake me for the next three weeks." And I *did* sleep, with a forty slumber-power; and when F. came to me late in the evening with some tea and toast, I awoke, oh! *so* refreshed, and perfectly well, for, after all the great fuss which I had made, there was nothing the matter with me but a little fatigue.

Every one that we met congratulated us upon not having encountered any Indians, for the paths which we followed were Indian trails, and it is said they would have killed us for our mules and clothes. A few weeks ago a Frenchman and his wife were murdered by them. I had thought of the circumstances when we camped, but was too sick to care what happened. They generally take women captive, however; and who knows how narrowly I escaped becoming an Indian chieftainess, and feeding for the rest of my life upon roasted grasshoppers, acorns, and flower-seeds? By the way, the last-mentioned article of food strikes me as rather poetical than otherwise.

After a good night's rest we are perfectly well, and as happy as the day itself,—which was one of Heaven's own choosing,—and rode to the "Wild Yankee's," where we breakfasted, and had, among other dainties, fresh butter and cream.

Soon after we alighted, a *herd* of Indians, consisting of about a dozen men and squaws, with an unknown quantity of papooses,—the last naked as the day they were born,—crowded into the room to stare at us. It was the most amusing thing in the world to see them finger my gloves, whip, and hat, in their intense curiosity. One of them had caught the following line of a song, "O, carry me back to old Martinez," with which he continued to stun our ears all the time we remained, repeating it over and over with as much pride and joy as a mocking-bird exhibits when he has learned a new sound.

On this occasion I was more than ever struck with what I have often remarked before,—the extreme beauty of the *limbs* of the Indian women of California. Though for haggardness of expression and ugliness of feature they might have been taken for a band of Macbethian witches, a bronze statue of Cleopatra herself never folded more beautifully rounded arms above its dusky bosom, or poised upon its pedestal a slenderer ankle or a more statuesque foot, than those which gleamed from beneath the dirty blankets of these wretched creatures. There was one exception, however, to the general hideousness of their faces. A girl of sixteen, perhaps, with those large, magnificently lustrous, yet at the same time soft, eyes, so common in novels, so rare in real life, had shyly glided like a dark, beautiful spirit into the corner of the room. A fringe of silken jet swept heavily upward from her dusky cheek, athwart which the richest color came and went like flashes of lightning. Her flexible lips curved slightly away from teeth like strips of cocoanut meat, with a mocking grace infinitely bewitching. She wore a cotton chemise,—disgustingly dirty, I must confess,—girt about her slender waist with a crimson handkerchief, while over her night-black hair, carelessly knotted beneath the rounded chin, was a purple scarf of knotted silk. Her whole appearance was picturesque in the extreme. She sat upon the ground with her pretty brown fingers languidly interlaced above her knee, "round as a *period*," (as a certain American poet has so funnily said of a similar limb in his Diana,) and smiled up into my face as if we were the dearest friends.

I was perfectly enraptured with this wildwood Cleopatra, and bored F. almost beyond endurance with exclamations about her starry eyes, her chiseled limbs, and her beautiful nut-brown cheeks.

I happened to take out of my pocket a paper of pins, when all the women begged for some of them. This lovely child still remained silent in the posture of exquisite grace which she had so unconsciously assumed, but, nevertheless, she looked as pleased as any of them when I gave her, also, a row of the much-coveted treasures. But I found I had got myself into business, for all the men wanted pins too, and I distributed the entire contents of the papers which I happened to have in my pocket, before they were satisfied, much to the amusement of F., who only laughs at what he is pleased to call my absurd interest in these poor creatures; but you know, M., I always *did* "take" to Indians, though it must be said that those who bear that name here have little resemblance to the glorious forest heroes that live in the Leatherstocking tales, and in spite of my desire to find in them something poetical and interesting, a stern regard for truth compels me to acknowledge that the dusky beauty above described is the only even moderately *pretty* squaw that I have ever seen.

At noon we stopped at the Buckeye Rancho for about an hour, and then pushed merrily on for the Pleasant Valley Rancho, which we expected to reach about sundown. Will you, *can* you, believe that we got lost again? Should you travel over this road, you would not be at all surprised at the repetition of this misfortune. Two miles this side of Pleasant Valley, which is very large, there is a wide, bare plain of red stones which one is compelled to cross in order to reach it, and I should not think that even in the daytime any one but an Indian could keep the trail in this place. It was here that, just at dark, we probably missed the path, and entered, about the center of the valley, at the opposite side of an extensive grove from that on which the rancho is situated. When I first began to suspect that we might possibly have to camp out another night, I Caudleized at a great rate, but when it became a fixed fact that such was our fate, I was instantly as mute and patient as the Widow Prettyman when she succeeded to the throne of the venerated woman referred to above. Indeed, feeling perfectly well, and not being much fatigued, I should rather have enjoyed it, had not F., poor fellow, been so grieved at the idea of my going supperless to a moss-stuffed couch. It was a long time before I could coax him to give up searching for the rancho, and, in truth, I should think that we rode round that part of the valley in which we found ourselves, for more than two hours, trying to find it.

About eleven o'clock we went back into the woods and camped for the night. Our bed was quite comfortable, and my saddle made an excellent pillow. Being so much higher in the mountains, we were a little chilly, and I was disturbed two or three times by a distant noise, which I have since been told was the growling of grizzly bears, that abounded in that vicinity. On the whole, we passed a comfortable night, and rose at sunrise feeling perfectly refreshed and well. In less than an hour we were eating breakfast at the Pleasant Valley Rancho, which we easily discovered by daylight.

Here they informed us that "we had escaped a great marcy," as old Jim used to say in relating his successful run from a wolf, inasmuch as the grizzlies had not devoured us during the night! But, seriously, dear M., my heart thrills with gratitude to the Father for his tender care of us during that journey, which, view it as lightly as we may, was certainly attended with *some* danger.

Notwithstanding we had endured so much fatigue, I felt as well as ever I did, and after breakfast insisted upon pursuing our journey, although F. anxiously advised me to defer it until next day. But imagine the horror, the *crème de la crème* of borosity, of remaining for twelve mortal hours of wakefulness in a filthy, uncomfortable, flea-haunted shanty, without books or papers, when Rich Bar—easily attainable before night, through the loveliest scenery, shining in the yellow splendor of an autumnal morn—lay before us! *I* had no idea of any such absurd self-immolation. So we again started on our strange, eventful journey.

I wish I could give you some faint idea of the majestic solitudes through which we passed,—where the pine-trees rise so grandly in their awful height, that they seem to look into heaven itself. Hardly a living thing disturbed this solemnly beautiful wilderness. Now and then a tiny lizard glanced in and out among the mossy roots of the old trees, or a golden butterfly flitted languidly from blossom to blossom. Sometimes a saucy little squirrel would gleam along the somber trunk of some ancient oak, or a bevy of quail, with their pretty tufted heads and short, quick tread, would trip athwart our path. Two or three times, in the radiant distance, we descried a stately deer, which, framed in by embowering leaves, and motionless as a tableau, gazed at us for a moment with its large, limpid eyes, and then bounded away with the speed of light into the evergreen depths of those glorious old woods.

Sometimes we were compelled to cross broad plains, acres in extent, called chaparrals, covered with low shrubs, which, leafless and barkless, stand like vegetable skeletons along the dreary waste. You cannot imagine what a weird effect these eldrich bushes had upon my mind. Of a ghastly whiteness, they at first reminded me of a plantation of antlers, and I amused myself by fancying them a herd of crouching deer; but they grew so wan and ghastly, that I began to look forward to the creeping across a chaparral (it is no easy task for the mules to wind through them) with almost a feeling of dread.

But what a lovely sight greeted our enchanted eyes as we stopped for a few moments on the summit of the hill leading into Rich Bar! Deep in the shadowy nooks of the far-down valleys, like wasted jewels dropped from the radiant sky above, lay half a dozen blue-bosomed lagoons, glittering and gleaming and sparkling in the sunlight as though each tiny wavelet were formed of rifted diamonds. It was worth the whole wearisome journey—danger from Indians, grizzly bears, sleeping under the stars, and all—to behold this beautiful vision. While I stood breathless with admiration, a singular sound, and an exclamation of "A rattlesnake!" from F., startled me into common sense again. I gave one look at the reptile, horribly beautiful, like a chain of living opals, as it corkscrewed itself into that peculiar spiral which it is compelled to assume in order to make an attack, and then, fear overcoming curiosity, although I had never seen one of them before, I galloped out of its vicinity as fast as my little mule could carry me.

The hill leading into Rich Bar is five miles long, and as steep as you can imagine. Fancy yourself riding for this distance along the edge of a frightful precipice, where, should your mule make a misstep, you would be dashed hundreds of feet into the awful ravine below. Every one we met tried to discourage us, and said that it would be impossible for me to ride down it. They would take F. aside, much to my amusement, and tell him that he was assuming a great responsibility in allowing me to undertake such a journey. I, however, insisted upon going on. About halfway down we came to a level spot, a few feet in extent, covered with sharp slate-stones. Here the girth of my saddle, which we afterwards found to be fastened only by four *tacks*, gave way, and I fell over the right side, striking on my left elbow. Strange to say, I was not in the least hurt, and again my heart wept tearful thanks to God, for, had the accident happened at any other part of the hill, I must have been dashed, a piece of shapeless nothingness, into the dim valleys beneath.

F. soon mended the saddle-girth. I mounted my darling little mule, and rode triumphantly into Rich Bar at five o'clock in the evening. The Rich Barians are astonished at my courage in daring to ride down the hill. Many of the miners have told me that they dismounted several times while descending it. I, of course, feel very vain of my exploit, and glorify myself accordingly, being particularly careful, all the time, not to inform my admirers that my courage was the result of the know-nothing, fear-nothing principle; for I was certainly ignorant, until I had passed them, of the dangers of the passage. Another thing that prevented my dismounting was the apparently utter impossibility, on such a steep and narrow path, of mounting again. Then, I had much more confidence in my mule's power of picking the way and keeping his footing, than in my own. It is the prettiest sight in the world to see these cunning creatures stepping so daintily and cautiously among the rocks. Their pretty little feet, which absolutely do not look larger than a silver dollar, seem made on purpose for the task. They are often perfect little vixens with their masters, but an old mountaineer, who has ridden them for twenty years, told me that he never knew one to be skittish with a woman. The intelligent darlings seem to know what a bundle of helplessness they are carrying, and scorn to take advantage of it.

We are boarding, at present, at the "Empire," a huge shingle palace in the center of Rich Bar, which I will describe in my next letter. Pardon, dear M., the excessive egotism of this letter; but you have often flattered me by saying that my epistles were only interesting when profusely illuminated by that manuscriptal decoration represented by a great *I*. A most intense love of the ornament myself makes it easy for me to believe you, and doubt not that my future communications will be as profusely stained with it as even you could desire.

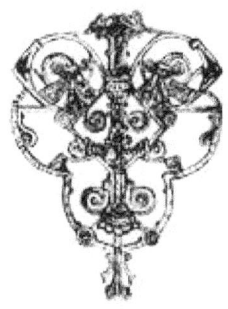

Letter the Second

[The Pioneer, March, 1854]

RICH BAR—ITS HOTELS and PIONEER FAMILIES

SYNOPSIS

The Empire Hotel, *the* hotel of Rich Bar. The author safely ensconced therein. California might be called the "Hotel State," from the plenitude of its taverns, etc. The Empire the only two-story building in Rich Bar, and the only one there having glass windows. Built by gamblers for immoral purposes. The speculation a failure, its occupants being treated with contempt or pity. Building sold for a few hundred dollars. The new landlord of the Empire. The landlady, an example of the terrible wear and tear to the complexion in crossing the plains. A resolute woman. Left behind her two children and an eight-months-old baby. Cooking for six people, her two-weeks-old baby kicking and screaming in champagne-basket cradle.

"The sublime martyrdom of maternity". Left alone immediately after infant's birth. Husband dangerously ill, and cannot help. A kindly miner. Three other women at the Bar. The "Indiana girl". "Girl" a misnomer.

"A gigantic piece of humanity". "Dainty" habits and herculean feats. A log-cabin family. Pretty and interesting children. "The Miners' Home". Its petite landlady tends bar. "Splendid material for social parties this winter."

Letter the Second

Rich Bar—Its Hotels and Pioneer Families

Rich Bar, East Branch of the North Fork of Feather River,

September 15, 1851.

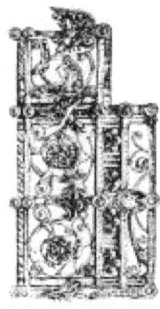

I believe that I closed my last letter by informing you that I was safely ensconced—after all the hair-breadth escapes of my wearisome, though at the same time delightful, journey—under the magnificent roof of the "Empire," which, by the way, is *the* hotel of the place, not but that nearly ever other shanty on the Bar claims the same grandiloquent title. Indeed, for that matter, California herself might be called the Hotel State, so completely is she inundated with taverns, boarding-houses, etc. The Empire is the only two-story building in town, and absolutely has a live "upstairs." Here you will find two or three glass windows, an unknown luxury in all the other dwellings. It is built of planks of the roughest possible description. The roof, of course, is covered with canvas, which also forms the entire front of the house, on which is painted, in immense capitals, the following imposing letters: "THE EMPIRE!" I will describe, as exactly as possible, this grand establishment. You first enter a large apartment, level with the street, part of which is fitted up as a barroom, with that eternal crimson calico which flushes the whole social life of the Golden State with its everlasting red, in the center of a fluted mass of which gleams a really elegant mirror, set off by a background of decanters, cigar-vases, and jars of brandied fruit; the whole forming a *tout ensemble*

of dazzling splendor. A table covered with a green cloth,—upon which lies a pack of monte-cards, a back-gammon-board, and a sickening pile of "yellow-kivered" literature,—with several uncomfortable-looking benches, complete the furniture of this most important portion of such a place as "The Empire." The remainder of the room does duty as a shop, where velveteen and leather, flannel shirts and calico ditto,—the latter starched to an appalling state of stiffness,—lie cheek by jowl with hams, preserved meats, oysters, and other groceries, in hopeless confusion. From the barroom you ascend by four steps into the parlor, the floor of which is covered by a straw carpet. This room contains quite a decent looking-glass, a sofa fourteen feet long and a foot and a half wide, painfully suggestive of an aching back,—of course covered with red calico (the sofa, *not* the back),—a round table with a green cloth, six cane-bottom chars, red-calico curtains, a cooking-stove, a rocking-chair, *and* a woman and a baby, (of whom more anon,) the latter wearing a scarlet frock, to match the sofa and curtains. A flight of four steps leads from the parlor to the upper story, where, on each side of a narrow entry, are four eight-feet-by-ten bedrooms, the floors of which are covered by straw matting. Here your eyes are again refreshed with a glittering vision of red-calico curtains gracefully festooned above wooden windows picturesquely lattice-like. These tiny chambers are furnished with little tables covered with oilcloth, and bedsteads so heavy that nothing short of a giant's strength could move them. Indeed, I am convinced that they were built, piece by piece, on the spot where they now stand. The entire building is lined with purple calico, alternating with a delicate blue, and the effect is really quite pretty. The floors are so very uneven that you are always ascending a hill or descending into a valley. The doors consist of a slight frame covered with dark-blue drilling, and are hung on hinges of leather. As to the kitchen and dining-room, I leave to your vivid imagination to picture their primitiveness, merely observing that nothing was ever more awkward and unworkmanlike than the whole tenement. It is just such a piece of carpentering as a child two years old, gifted with the strength of a man, would produce, if it wanted to play at making grown-up houses. And yet this impertinent apology for a house cost its original owners more than eight thousand dollars. This will not be quite so surprising when I inform you that, at the time it was built, everything had to be packed from Marysville at a cost of forty cents a pound. Compare this with the price of freight on the railroads at home, and you will easily make an estimate of the immense outlay of money necessary to collect the materials for such an undertaking at Rich Bar. It was built by a company of gamblers as a residence for two of those unfortunates who make a trade—a thing of barter—of the holiest passion, when sanctified by *love*, that ever thrills the wayward heart of poor humanity. To the lasting honor of *miners* be it written, the *speculation* proved a decided failure. Yes! these thousand men, many of whom had been for years absent from the softening amenities of female society, and the sweet restraining influences of pure womanhood,—these husbands of fair young wives kneeling daily at the altars of their holy homes to pray for their far-off ones,— these sons of gray-haired mothers, majestic in their sanctified old age,—these brothers of virginal sisters, white and saintlike as the lilies of their own gardens,—looked only with contempt or pity on these, oh! so earnestly to be compassionated creatures. These unhappy members of a class, to one of which the tenderest words that Jesus ever spake were uttered, left in a few weeks, absolutely driven away by public opinion. The disappointed gamblers sold the house to its present proprietor for a few hundred dollars.

Mr. B., the landlord of the Empire, was a Western farmer who with his wife crossed the plains about two years ago. Immediately on his arrival he settled at a mining station, where he remained until last spring, when he removed to Rich Bar. Mrs. B. is a gentle and amiable looking woman, about twenty-five years of age. She is an example of the terrible wear and tear to the complexion in crossing the plains, hers having become, through exposure at that time, of a dark and permanent yellow, anything but becoming. I will give you a key to her character, which will exhibit it better than weeks of description. She took a nursing babe, eight months old, from her bosom, and left it with two other children, almost infants, to cross the plains in search of gold! When I arrived she was cooking supper for some half a dozen people, while her really pretty boy, who lay kicking furiously in his champagne-basket cradle, and screaming with a six-months-old-baby power, had, that day, completed just two weeks of his earthly pilgrimage. The inconvenience which she suffered during what

George Sand calls "the sublime martyrdom of maternity" would appal the wife of the humblest pauper of a New England village. Another woman, also from the West, was with her at the time of her infant's birth, but scarcely had the "latest-found" given the first characteristic shriek of its debut upon the stage of life, when this person herself was taken seriously ill, and was obliged to return to her own cabin, leaving the poor exhausted mother entirely alone! Her husband lay seriously sick himself at the time, and of course could offer her no assistance. A miner, who lived in the house, and hoarded himself, carried her some bread and tea in the morning and evening, and that was all the care she had. Two days after its birth, she made a desperate effort, and, by easy stages of ten minutes at a time, contrived to get poor baby washed and dressed, after a fashion. He is an astonishingly large and strong child, holds his head up like a six-monther, and has but one failing,—a too evident and officious desire to inform everybody, far and near, at all hours of the night and day, that his lungs are in a perfectly sound and healthy condition,—a piece of intelligence which, though very gratifying, is rather inconvenient if one happens to be particularly sleepy.

Besides Mrs. B., there are three other women on the Bar. One is called "the Indiana girl," from the name of her pa's hotel, though it must be confessed that the sweet name of *girl* seems sadly incongruous when applied to such a gigantic piece of humanity. I have a great desire to see her, which will probably not be gratified, as she leaves in a few days for the valley. But, at any rate, I can say that I have *heard* her. The far-off roll of her mighty voice, booming through two closed doors and a long entry, added greatly to the severe attack of nervous headache under which I was suffering when she called. This gentle creature wears the thickest kind of miner's boots, and has the dainty habit of wiping the dishes on her apron! Last spring she *walked* to this place, and packed fifty pounds of flour on her back down that awful hill, the snow being five feet deep at the time.

Mr. and Mrs. B., who have three pretty children, reside in a log cabin at the entrance of the village. One of the little girls was in the barroom to-day, and her sweet and birdlike voice brought tearfully, and yet joyfully, to my memory "Tearsoul," "Leilie," and "Lile Katie."

Mrs. B., who is as small as "the Indiana girl" is large (indeed, I have been confidently informed that she weighs but sixty-eight pounds), keeps, with her husband, the "Miners' Home." (Mem.—The lady tends bar.) *Voilà*, my dear, the female population of my new home. Splendid material for social parties this winter, are they not?

Letter the Third

[The Pioneer, April, 1854]

LIFE and FORTUNE at the BAR-DIGGINGS

SYNOPSIS

Flashy shops and showy houses of San Francisco. Rich Bar charmingly fresh and original. A diminutive valley. Río de las Plumas, or Feather River. Rich Bar, the Barra Rica of the Spaniards. An acknowledgment of "a most humiliating consciousness of geological deficiencies". Palatial splendor of the Empire Hotel. Round tents, square tents, plank hovels, log cabins, etc. "Local habitations" formed of pine boughs, and covered with old calico shirts. The "office" of Dr. C. excites the risibilities of the author. One of the "finders" of Rich Bar. Had not spoken to a woman for two years. Honors the occasion by an "investment" in champagne. The author assists in drinking to the honor of her arrival at the Bar. Nothing done in California without the sanctifying influence of the "spirit". History of the discovery of gold at Rich Bar. Thirty-three pounds of gold in eight hours. Fifteen hundred dollars from a panful of "dirt". Five hundred miners arrive at Rich Bar in about a week. Smith Bar, Indian Bar, Missouri Bar, and other bars. Miners extremely fortunate. Absolute wealth in a few weeks. Drunken gamblers in less than a year. Suffering for necessaries of life. A mild winter. A stormy spring. Impassable trails. No pack-mule trains arrive. Miners pack flour on their backs for over forty miles. Flour at over three dollars a pound. Subsistence on feed-barley. A voracious miner. An abundance stored.

Letter the Third
Life and Fortune at the Bar-diggings
Rich Bar, East Branch of the North Fork of Feather River,
September 20, 1851.

I intend, to-day, dear M., to be as disagreeably statistical and as praiseworthily matter-of-factish as the most dogged utilitarian could desire. I shall give you a full, true, and particular account of the discovery, rise, and progress of this place, with a religious adherence to *dates* which will rather astonish your unmathematical mind. But let me first describe the spot as it looked to my wondering and unaccustomed eyes. Remember, I had never seen a mining district before, and had just left San Francisco, amid whose flashy-looking shops and showy houses the most of my time had been spent since my arrival in the Golden State. Of course, to me, the *coup d'oeil* of Rich Bar was charmingly fresh and original. Imagine a tiny valley about eight hundred yards in length, and perhaps thirty in width, (it was measured for my especial information,) apparently hemmed in by lofty hills, almost perpendicular, draperied to their very summits with beautiful fir-trees, the blue-bosomed Plumas (or Feather River, I suppose I must call it) undulating along their base,—and you have as good an idea as I can give you of the *local* of Barra Rica, as the Spaniards so prettily term it.

In almost any of the numerous books written upon California, no doubt you will be able to find a most scientific description of the origin of these bars. I must acknowledge with shame that my ideas on the subject are distressingly vague. I could never appreciate the poetry or the humor of making one's wrists ache by knocking to pieces gloomy-looking stones, or in dirtying one's fingers by analyzing soils, in a vain attempt to fathom the osteology or anatomy of our beloved earth, though my heart is thrillingly alive to the faintest shade of color and the infinite variety of styles in which she delights to robe her ever-changeful and ever-beautiful *surface*. In my unscientific mind, the *formations* are without form, and void; and you might as well talk Chinese to me, as to embroider your conversation with the terms "hornblende," "mica," "limestone," "slate," "granite," and "quartz" in a hopeless attempt to enlighten me as to their merits. The dutiful diligence with which I attended course after course of lectures on geology, by America's greatest illustrator of that subject, arose rather from my affectionate reverence for our beloved Dr. H., and the fascinating charm which his glorious mind throws round every subject which it condescends to illuminate, than to any interest in the dry science itself. It is therefore with a most humiliating consciousness of my geological deficiencies that I offer you the only explanation which I have been able to obtain from those most learned in such matters here. I gather from their remarks, that these bars are formed by deposits of earth rolling down from the mountains, crowding the river aside and occupying a portion of its deserted bed. If my definition is unsatisfactory, I can but refer you to some of the aforesaid works upon California.

Through the middle of Rich Bar runs the street, thickly planted with about forty tenements, among which figure round tents, square tents, plank hovels, log cabins, etc., the residences varying in elegance and convenience from the palatial splendor of "The Empire" down to a "local habitation" formed of pine boughs and covered with old calico shirts.

To-day I visited the "office," the only one on the river. I had heard so much about it from others, as well as from F., that I really *did* expect something extra. When I entered this imposing place the shock to my optic nerves was so great that I sank helplessly upon one of the benches, which ran, divan-like, the whole length (ten feet!) of the building, and laughed till I cried. There was, of course, no floor. A rude nondescript, in one corner, on which was ranged the medical library, consisting of half a dozen volumes, did duty as a table. The shelves, which looked like sticks snatched hastily from the woodpile, and nailed up without the least alteration, contained quite a respectable array of medicines. The white-canvas window stared everybody in the face, with the interesting information painted on it, in perfect grenadiers of capitals, that this was Dr. ——'s office.

At my loud laugh (which, it must be confessed, was noisy enough to give the whole street assurance of the presence of a woman) F. looked shocked, and his partner looked prussic acid. To him (the partner, I mean; he hadn't been out of the mines for years) the "office" was a thing sacred, and set apart for an almost admiring worship. It was a beautiful architectural ideal embodied in pine shingles and cotton cloth. Here he literally "lived, and moved, and had his being," his bed and his board. With an admiration of the fine arts truly praiseworthy, he had fondly decorated the walls thereof with sundry pictures from Godey's, Graham's, and Sartain's magazines, among which, fashion-plates with imaginary monsters sporting miraculous waists, impossible wrists, and fabulous feet, largely predominated.

During my call at the office I was introduced to one of the *finders* of Rich Bar,—a young Georgian,—who afterwards gave me a full description of all the facts connected with its discovery. This unfortunate had not spoken to a woman for two years, and, in the elation of his heart at the joyful event, he rushed out and invested capital in some excellent champagne, which I, on Willie's principle of "doing in Turkey as the Turkeys do," assisted the company in drinking, to the honor of my own arrival. I mention this as an instance that nothing can be done in California without the sanctifying influence of the *spirit*, and it generally appears in a much more "questionable shape" than that of sparkling wine. Mr. H. informed me that on the 20th of July, 1850, it was rumored at Nelson's Creek—a mining station situated at the Middle Fork of the Feather River, about eighty miles from Marysville—that one of those vague "Somebodies," a near relation of the "They-Says," had discovered mines of a remarkable richness in a northeasterly direction, and about forty miles from the first-mentioned place. Anxious and immediate search was made for "Somebody," but, as our Western brethren say, he "wasn't thar'." But his absence could not deter the miners when once the golden rumor had been set afloat. A large company packed up their goods and chattels, generally consisting of a pair of blankets, a frying-pan, some flour, salt pork, brandy, pickax and shovel, and started for the new Dorado. They "traveled, and traveled, and traveled," as we used to say in the fairy-stories, for nearly a week, in every possible direction, when, one evening, weary and discouraged, about one hundred of the party found themselves at the top of that famous hill which figures so largely in my letters, whence the river can be distinctly seen. Half of the number concluded to descend the mountain that night, the remainder stopping on the summit until the next morning. On arriving at Rich Bar, part of the adventurers camped there, but many went a few miles farther down the river. The next morning, two men turned over a large stone, beneath which they found quite a sizable piece of gold. They washed a small panful of the dirt, and obtained from it two hundred and fifty-six dollars. Encouraged by this success, they commenced staking off the legal amount of ground allowed to each person for mining purposes, and, the remainder of the party having descended the hill, before night the entire bar was "claimed." In a fortnight from that time, the two men who found the first bit of gold had each taken out six thousand dollars. Two others took out thirty-three pounds of gold in eight hours, which is the best day's work that has been done on this branch of the river. The largest amount ever taken from one panful of dirt was fifteen hundred dollars. In a little more than a week after its discovery, five hundred men had settled upon the Bar for the summer. Such is the wonderful alacrity with which a mining town is built. Soon after was discovered, on the same side of the river, about half a mile apart, and at nearly the same distance from this place, the two bars, Smith and Indian, both very rich, also another, lying across the river, just opposite Indian, called Missouri Bar. There are several more, all within a few miles of here, called Frenchman's, Taylor's, Brown's, The Junction, Wyandott, and Muggin's; but they are, at present, of little importance as mining stations.

Those who worked in these mines during the fall of 1850 were extremely fortunate, but, alas! the monte fiend ruined hundreds. Shall I tell you the fate of two of the most successful of these gold-hunters?

From poor men, they found themselves, at the end of a few weeks, absolutely rich. Elated with their good fortune, seized with a mania for monte, in less than a year these unfortunates, so lately respectable and intelligent, became a pair of drunken gamblers. One of them, at this present writing, works for five dollars a day, and boards himself out of that; the other actually suffers for the necessaries of life,—a too common result of scenes in the mines.

There were but few that dared to remain in the mountains during the winter, for fear of being buried in the snow, of which, at that time, they had a most vague idea. I have been told that in these sheltered valleys it seldom falls to the depth of more than a foot, and disappears almost invariably within a day or two. Perhaps there were three hundred that concluded to stay, of which number two thirds stopped on Smith's Bar, as the labor of mining there is much easier than it is here. Contrary to the general expectation, the weather was delightful until about the middle of March. It then commenced storming, and continued to snow and rain incessantly for nearly three weeks. Supposing that the rainy season had passed, hundreds had arrived on the river during the previous month. The snow, which fell several feet in depth on the mountains, rendered the trail impassable, and entirely stopped the pack trains. Provisions soon became scarce, and the sufferings of these unhappy men were indeed extreme. Some adventurous spirits, with true Yankee hardihood, forced their way through the snow to the Frenchman's rancho, and packed flour *on their backs* for more than forty miles! The first meal that arrived sold for three dollars a pound. Many subsisted for days on nothing but barley, which is kept here to feed the pack-mules on. One unhappy individual, who could not obtain even a little barley for love or money, and had eaten nothing for three days, forced his way out to the Spanish Rancho, fourteen miles distant, and in less than an hour after his arrival had devoured *twenty-seven* biscuit and a corresponding quantity of other eatables, and, of course, drinkables to match. Don't let this account alarm you. There is no danger of another famine here. They tell me that there is hardly a building in the place that has not food enough in it to last its occupants for the next two years; besides, there are two or three well-filled groceries in town

Letter the Fourth

[The Pioneer, May, 1854]

ACCIDENTS—SURGERY—DEATH—FESTIVITY

SYNOPSIS

Frightful accidents to which the gold-seeker is constantly liable. Futile attempts of physician to save crushed leg of young miner. Universal outcry against amputation. Dr. C., however, uses the knife. Professional reputation at stake. Success attends the operation. Death of another young miner, who fell into mining-shaft. His funeral. Picturesque appearance of the miners thereat. Of what the miner's costume consists. Horror of the author aroused in contemplation of the lonely mountain-top graveyard. Jostling of life and death. Celebration of the anniversary of Chilian independence. Participation of a certain class of Yankees therein. The procession. A Falstaffian leader. The feast. A twenty-gallon keg of brandy on the table, gracefully encircled by quart dippers. The Chileños reel with a better grace, the Americans more naturally.

Letter the Fourth
Accidents—Surgery—Death—Festivity
Rich Bar, East Branch of the North Fork of Feather River,
September 22, 1851.

 There has been quite an excitement here for the last week, on account of a successful amputation having been performed upon the person of a young man by the name of W. As I happen to know all the circumstances of the case, I will relate them to you as illustrative of the frightful accidents to which the gold-seekers are constantly liable, and I can assure you that similar ones happen very often. W. was one of the first who settled on this river, and suffered extremely from the scarcity of provisions during the last winter. By steady industry in his laborious vocation, he had accumulated about four thousand dollars. He was thinking seriously of returning to Massachusetts with what he had already gained, when, in the early part of last May, a stone, unexpectedly rolling from the top of Smith's Hill, on the side of which he was mining, crushed his leg in the most shocking manner. Naturally enough, the poor fellow shrank with horror from the idea of an amputation here in the mountains. It seemed absolutely worse than death. His physician, appreciating his feelings on the subject, made every effort to save his shattered limb, but, truly, the Fates seemed against him. An attack of typhoid fever reduced him to a state of great weakness, which was still further increased by erysipelas—a common complaint in the mountains—in its most virulent form. The latter disease, settling in the fractured leg, rendered a cure utterly hopeless. His sufferings have

been of the most intense description. Through all the blossoming spring, and a summer as golden as its own golden self, of our beautiful California he has languished away existence in a miserable cabin, his only nurses men, some of them, it is true, kind and good, others neglectful and careless. A few weeks since, F. was called in to see him. He decided immediately that nothing but an amputation would save him. A universal outcry against it was raised by nearly all the other physicians on the Bar.

They agreed, *en masse*, that he could live but a few weeks unless the leg—now a mere lump of disease—was taken off. At the same time, they declared that he would certainly expire under the knife, and that it was cruel to subject him to any further suffering. You can perhaps imagine F.'s anxiety. It was a great responsibility for a young physician to take. Should the patient die during the operation, F.'s professional reputation would, of course, die with him; but he felt it his duty to waive all selfish considerations, and give W. that one chance, feeble as it seemed, for his life. Thank God, the result was most triumphant. For several days existence hung upon a mere thread. He was not allowed to speak or move, and was fed from a teaspoon, his only diet being milk, which we obtained from the Spanish Rancho, sending twice a week for it. I should have mentioned that F. decidedly refused to risk an operation in the small and miserable tent in which W. had languished away nearly half a year, and he was removed to the Empire the day previous to the amputation. It is almost needless to tell you that the little fortune, to accumulate which he suffered so much, is now nearly exhausted. Poor fellow! the philosophy and cheerful resignation with which he has endured his terrible martyrdom is beautiful to behold. My heart aches as I look upon his young face and think of "his gentle dark-eyed mother weeping lonely at the North" for her far-away and suffering son.

As I sat by the bedside of our poor invalid, yielding myself up to a world of dreamy visionings suggested by the musical sweep of the pine branch which I waved above his head, and the rosy sunset flushing the western casement with its soft glory, he suddenly opened his languid eyes and whispered, "The Chileño procession is returning. Do you not hear it?" I did not tell him—

That the weary sound, and the heavy breath,
And the silent motions of passing death,
And the smell, cold, oppressive, and dank,
Sent through the pores of the coffin-plank,

had already informed me that a far other band than that of the noisy South Americans was solemnly marching by. It was the funeral train of a young man who was instantly killed, the evening before, by falling into one of those deep pits, sunk for mining purposes, which are scattered over the Bar in almost every direction. I rose quietly and looked from the window. About a dozen persons were carrying an unpainted coffin, without pall or bier (the place of the latter being supplied by ropes), up the steep hill which rises behind the Empire, on the top of which is situated the burial-ground of Rich Bar. The bearers were all neatly and cleanly dressed in their miner's costume, which, consisting of a flannel shirt (almost always of a dark-blue color), pantaloons with the boots drawn up over them, and a low-crowned broad-brimmed black felt hat (though the fashion of the latter is not invariable), is not, simple as it seems, so unpicturesque as you might perhaps imagine. A strange horror of that lonely mountain graveyard came over me as I watched the little company wending wearily up to the solitary spot. The "sweet habitude of being"—not that I fear *death*, but that I love *life* as, for instance, Charles Lamb loved it—makes me particularly affect a cheerful burial-place. I know that it is dreadfully unsentimental, but I should like to make my last home in the heart of a crowded city, or, better still, in one of those social homes of the dead, which the Turks, with a philosophy so beautiful and so poetical, make their most cheerful resort. Singularly enough, Christians seem to delight in rendering death particularly hideous, and graveyards decidedly disagreeable. I, on the contrary, would "plant the latter with laurels, and sprinkle it with lilies." I would wreathe "sleep's pale brother" so thickly with roses that even those rabid moralists who think that it makes us better to paint him as a dreadful fiend, instead of a loving friend, could see nothing but their blushing radiance. I would alter the whole paraphernalia of the coffin, the shroud, and the bier, particularly the first, which, as Dickens says, "looks like a high-shouldered ghost with its hands in its breeches-pockets." Why should we endeavor to make our entrance into a glorious immortality so unutterably ghastly? Let us glide into the "fair shadowland" through a "gate of flowers," if we may no longer, as in the majestic olden time, aspire heavenward on the wings of perfumed flame.

How oddly do life and death jostle each other in this strange world of ours! How nearly allied are smiles and tears! My eyes were yet moist from the egotistical *pitié de moi-même* in which I had been indulging at the thought of sleeping forever amid these lonely hills, which in a few years must return to their primeval solitude, perchance never again to be awakened by the voice of humanity, when the Chileño procession, every member of it most intensely drunk, really *did* appear. I never saw anything more diverting than the whole affair. Of course, *selon les règles*, I ought to have been shocked and horrified, to have shed salt tears, and have uttered melancholy jeremiads over their miserable degradation; but the world is so full of platitudes, my dear, that I think you will easily forgive me for not boring you with a temperance lecture, and will good-naturedly let me have my laugh, and not think me *very* wicked, after all.

You must know that to-day is the anniversary of the independence of Chile. The procession got up in honor of it consisted, perhaps, of twenty men, nearly a third of whom were of that class of Yankees who are particularly noisy and particularly conspicuous in all celebrations where it is each man's most onerous duty to get what is technically called "tight." The man who headed the procession was a complete comic poem in his own individual self. He was a person of Falstaffian proportions and coloring, and if a brandy-barrel ever *does* "come alive," and, donning a red shirt and buckskin trousers, betake itself to pedestrianism, it will look more like my hero than anything else that I can at present think of. With that affectionateness so peculiar to people when they arrive at the sentimental stage of intoxication, although it was with the greatest difficulty that he could sustain his own corporosity, he was tenderly trying to direct the zigzag footsteps of his companion, a little withered-up, weird-looking Chileño. Alas for the wickedness of human nature! The latter, whose drunkenness had taken a Byronic and misanthropical turn, rejected with the basest ingratitude these delicate attentions. Do not think that my incarnated brandy-cask was the only one of the party who did unto others as he would they should do unto him, for the entire band were officiously tendering to one another the same good-Samaritan-like assistance. I was not astonished at the Virginia-fence-like style of their marching when I heard a description of the feast of which they had partaken a few hours before. A friend of mine, who stepped into the tent where they were dining, said that the board—really, *board*—was arranged with a bottle of claret at each plate, and, after the cloth (metaphorically speaking, I mean, for table-linen is a mere myth in the mines) was removed, a twenty-gallon keg of brandy was placed in the center, with quart dippers gracefully encircling it, that each one might help himself as he pleased. Can you wonder, after that, that every man vied with his neighbor in illustrating Hogarth's line of beauty? It was impossible to tell which nation was the more gloriously drunk; but this I *will* say, even at the risk of being thought partial to my own beloved countrymen, That, though the Chileños reeled with a better grace, the Americans did it more *naturally*!

Letter the Fifth
[The Pioneer, June, 1854]
DEATH of a MOTHER—LIFE of PIONEER WOMEN
SYNOPSIS

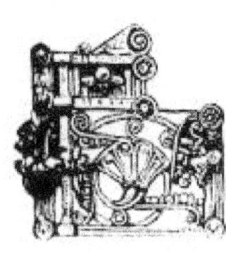

Death of one of the four pioneer women of Rich Bar. The funeral from the log-cabin residence. Sickly ten-months-old baby moans piteously for its mother. A handsome girl of sick years, unconscious of her bereavement, shocks the author by her actions. A monte-table cover as a funeral pall. Painful feelings when nails are driven into coffin. The extempore prayer. Every observance possible surrounded the funeral. Visit to a canvas house of three "apartments". Barroom, dining-room, kitchen with bed-closet. A sixty-eight-pound woman. "A magnificent woman, a wife of the right sort". "Earnt her 'old man' nine hundred dollars in nine weeks, by washing". The "manglers" and the "mangled". Fortitude of refined California women pioneers. The orphaned girl a "cold-blooded little wretch". Remorse of the author. "Baby decanters". The gayety and fearlessness of the orphaned girl.

Letter the Fifth

Death of a Mother—Life of Pioneer Women

Rich Bar, East Branch of the North Fork of Feather River,

September 22, 1851.

It seems indeed awful, dear M., to be compelled to announce to you the death of one of the four women forming the female population of this Bar. I have just returned from the funeral of poor Mrs. B., who died of peritonitis (a common disease in this place), after an illness of four days only. Our hostess herself heard of her sickness but two days since. On her return from a visit which she had paid to the invalid, she told me that although Mrs. B.'s family did not seem alarmed about her, in her opinion she would survive but a few hours. Last night we were startled by the frightful news of her decease. I confess that, without being very egotistical, the death of one, out of a community of four women, might well alarm the remainder.

Her funeral took place at ten this morning. The family reside in a log cabin at the head of the Bar, and although it has no window, all the light admitted entering through an aperture where there *will* be a door when it becomes cold enough for such a luxury, yet I am told, and can easily believe, that it is one of the most *comfortable* residences in the place. I observed it particularly, for it was the first log cabin that I had ever seen. Everything in the room, though of the humblest description, was exceedingly clean and neat.

On a board, supported by two butter-tubs, was extended the body of the dead woman, covered with a sheet. By its side stood the coffin, of unstained pine, lined with white cambric. You, who have alternately laughed and scolded at my provoking and inconvenient deficiency in the power of observing, will perhaps wonder at the minuteness of my descriptions; but I know how deeply you are interested in everything relating to California, and therefore I take pains to describe things exactly as I *see* them, hoping that thus you will obtain an idea of life in the mines *as it is.*

The bereaved husband held in his arms a sickly babe ten months old, which was moaning piteously for its mother. The other child, a handsome, bold-looking little girl six years of age, was running gayly around the room, perfectly unconscious of her great bereavement. A sickening horror came over me, to see her, every few moments, run up to her dead mother and peep laughingly under the handkerchief that covered her moveless face. Poor little thing! It was evident that her baby-toilet had been made by men. She had on a new calico dress, which, having no tucks in it, trailed to the floor, and gave her a most singular and dwarf-womanly appearance.

About twenty men, with the three women of the place, had assembled at the funeral. An extempore prayer was made, filled with all the peculiarities usual to that style of petition. Ah, how different from the soothing verses of the glorious burial service of the church!

As the procession started for the hillside graveyard, a dark cloth cover, borrowed from a neighboring monte-table, was flung over the coffin. Do not think that I mention any of these circumstances in a spirit of mockery. Far from it. Every observance usual on such occasions, that was *procurable*, surrounded this funeral. All the gold on Rich Bar could do no more; and should I die to-morrow, I should be marshaled to my mountain-grave beneath the same monte-table-cover pall which shrouded the coffin of poor Mrs. B.

I almost forgot to tell you how painfully the feelings of the assembly were shocked by the sound of the nails (there being no screws at any of the shops) driven with a hammer into the coffin while closing it. It seemed as if it *must* disturb the pale sleeper within.

To-day I called at the residence of Mrs. R. It is a canvas house containing a suite of three "apartments," as Dick Swiveller would say, which, considering that they were all on the ground-floor, are kept surprisingly neat. There is a barroom blushing all over with red calico, a dining-room, kitchen, and a small bed-closet. The little sixty-eight-pounder woman is queen of the establishment. By the way, a man who walked home with us was enthusiastic in her praise. "Magnificent woman, that, sir," he said, addressing my husband; "a wife of the right sort, *she* is. Why," he added, absolutely rising into eloquence as he spoke, "she earnt her *old man*" (said individual twenty-one years of age, perhaps) "nine hundred dollars in nine weeks, clear of all expenses, by washing! Such women ain't common, I tell *you*. If they were, a man might marry, and make money by the operation." I looked at this person with somewhat the same kind of *inverted* admiration wherewith Leigh Hunt was wont to gaze upon that friend of his "who used to elevate the commonplace to a pitch of the sublime," and he looked at *me* as if to say, that, though by no means gloriously arrayed, I was a mere cumberer of the ground, inasmuch as I toiled not, neither did I wash. Alas! I hung my diminished head, particularly when I remembered the eight dollars a dozen which I had been in the habit of paying for the washing of linen-cambric pocket-handkerchiefs while in San Francisco. But a lucky thought came into my mind. As all men cannot be Napoleon Bonapartes, so all women cannot be *manglers*. The majority of the sex must be satisfied with simply being *mangled*. Reassured by this idea, I determined to meekly and humbly pay the amount per dozen required to enable this really worthy and agreeable little woman "to lay up her hundred dollars a week, clear of expenses." But is it not wonderful what femininity is capable of? To look at the tiny hands of Mrs. R., you would not think it possible that they could wring out anything larger than a doll's nightcap; but, as is often said, nothing is strange in California. I have known of sacrifices requiring, it would seem, superhuman efforts, made by women in this country, who, at home, were nurtured in the extreme of elegance and delicacy.

Mr. B. called on us to-day with little Mary. I tried to make her, at least, look sad as I talked about her mother; but although she had seen the grave closed over her coffin (for a friend of her father's had carried her in his arms to the burial), she seemed laughingly indifferent to her loss. Being myself an orphan, my heart contracted painfully at her careless gayety when speaking of her dead parent, and I said to our hostess, "What a cold-blooded little wretch it is!" But immediately my conscience struck me with remorse. Poor orphaned one! Poor bereaved darling! Why should I so cruelly wish to darken her young life with that knowledge which a few years' experience will so painfully teach her? "All *my* mother came into my eyes" as I bent down and kissed the white lids which shrouded her beautiful dark orbs, and, taking her fat little hand in mine, I led her to my room, where, in the penitence of my heart, I gave her everything that she desired. The little chatterer was enchanted, not having had any new playthings for a long while. It was beautiful to hear her pretty exclamations of ecstasy at the sight of some tiny scent-bottles, about an inch in length, which she called baby decanters.

Mr. B. intends, in a day or two, to take his children to their grandmother, who resides somewhere near Marysville, I believe. This is an awful place for children, and nervous mothers would "die daily" if they could see little Mary running fearlessly to the very edge of, and looking down into, these holes (many of them sixty feet in depth), which have been excavated in the hope of finding gold, and of course left open.

Letter the Sixth
[The Pioneer, July, 1854]
USE of PROFANITY—UNCERTAINTY of MINING
SYNOPSIS

Prevalence of profanity in California. Excuses for its use. A mere slip of the tongue, etc. Grotesqueness of some blasphemous expressions. Sleep-killing mining machinery. What a flume is. Project to flume the river for many miles. The California mining system a gambling or lottery transaction. Miner who works his own claim the more successful. Dr. C. a loser in his mining ventures. Another sleep-killer. Bowling-alleys. Bizarre cant phrases and slang used by the miners "Honest Indian?" "Talk enough when horses fight". "Talk enough between gentlemen". "I've got the dead-wood on him". "I'm going nary cent" (on person mistrusted). All carry the freshness of originality to the author's ear.

Letter the Sixth

Use of Profanity—Uncertainty of Mining

Rich Bar, East Branch of the North Fork of Feather River, September 30, 1851.

I think that I have never spoken to you of the mournful extent to which profanity prevails in California. You know that at home it is considered *vulgar* for a gentleman to swear; but I am told that here it is absolutely the fashion, and that people who never uttered an oath in their lives while in the "States," now clothe themselves with curses as with a garment. Some try to excuse themselves by saying that it is a careless habit, into which they have glided imperceptibly from having been compelled to associate so long with the vulgar and the profane; that it is a mere slip of the tongue, which means absolutely nothing; etc. I am willing to believe this, and to think as charitably as possible of many persons here, who have unconsciously adopted a custom which I know they abhor. Whether there is more profanity in the mines than elsewhere, I know not; but, during the short time that I have been at Rich Bar, I have *heard* more of it than in all my life before. Of course the most vulgar blackguard will abstain from swearing in the *presence* of a lady, but in this rag-and-cardboard house one is *compelled* to hear the most sacred of names constantly profaned by the drinkers and gamblers, who haunt the barroom at all hours. And this is a custom which the gentlemanly and quiet proprietor, much as he evidently dislikes it, cannot possibly prevent. Some of these expressions, were they not so fearfully blasphemous, would be grotesquely sublime. For instance, not five minutes ago I heard two men quarreling in the street, and one said to the other,

"Only let me get hold of your beggarly carcass once, and I will use you up so small that God Almighty himself cannot see your *ghost*!"

To live thus, in constant danger of being hushed to one's rosy rest by a ghastly lullaby of oaths, is revolting in the extreme. For that reason, and because it is infinitely more comfortable during the winter season than a plank house, F. has concluded to build a log cabin, where, at least, I shall not be *obliged* to hear the solemn names of the Father and the dear Master so mockingly profaned.

But it is not the swearing alone which disturbs my slumber. There is a dreadful flume, the machinery of which keeps up the most dismal moaning and shrieking all the livelong night, painfully suggestive of a suffering child. But, O dear! you don't know what that is, do you? Now, if I were scientific, I should give you such a vivid description of it that you would see a pen-and-ink flume staring at you from this very letter. But, alas! my own ideas on the subject are in a state of melancholy vagueness. I will do the best possible, however, in the way of explanation. A flume, then, is an immense trough which takes up a portion of the river, and with the aid of a dam compels it to run in another channel, leaving the vacated bed of the stream ready for mining purposes.

There is a gigantic project now on the tapis, of fluming the entire river for many miles, commencing a little above Rich Bar. Sometimes these fluming companies are eminently successful; at others, their operations are a dead failure.

But, in truth, the whole mining system in California is one great gambling or, better perhaps, lottery transaction. It is impossible to tell whether a claim will prove valuable or not. F. has invariably sunk money in every one that he has bought. Of course a man who works a claim himself is more likely, even should it turn out poor, to get his money back, as they say, than one who, like F., hires it done.

A few weeks since, F. paid a thousand dollars for a claim which has proved utterly worthless. He might better have thrown his money into the river than to have bought it, and yet some of the most experienced miners on the Bar thought that it would pay.

But I began to tell you about the different noises which disturb my peace of mind by day and my repose of body by night, and have gone, instead, into a financial disquisition upon mining prospects. Pray forgive me, even though I confess that I intend, some day, when I feel statistically inclined, to bore you with some profound remarks upon the claiming, drifting, sluicing, ditching, fluming, and coyoting politics of the "diggins."

But to return to my sleep-murderers. The rolling on the bowling-alley never leaves off for ten consecutive minutes at any time during the entire twenty-four hours. It is a favorite amusement at the mines, and the only difference that Sunday makes is, that then it never leaves off for *one* minute.

Besides the flume and the bowling-alley, there is an inconsiderate dog which *will* bark from starry eve till dewy morn. I fancy that he has a wager on the subject, as all the other *puppies* seem bitten by the betting mania.

Apropos of dogs, I found dear old Dake, the noble Newfoundland which H. gave us, look as intensely black and as grandly aristocratical as ever. He is the only high-bred dog on the river. There is another animal, by the plebeian name of John (what a name for a *dog*!), really a handsome creature, which looks as if he might have a faint sprinkling of good blood in his veins. Indeed, I have thought it possible that his great-grandfather was a bulldog. But he always barks at *me*, which I consider as proof positive that he is nothing but a low-born mongrel. To be sure, his master says, to excuse him, that he never saw a woman before; but a dog of any chivalry would have recognized the gentler sex, even if it *was* the first time that he had been blessed with the sight.

In the first part of my letter I alluded to the swearing propensities of the Rich Barians. Those, of course, would shock you; but, though you hate slang, I know that you could not help smiling at some of their bizarre cant phrases.

For instance, if you tell a Rich Barian anything which he doubts, instead of simply asking you if it is true, he will *invariably* cock his head interrogatively, and almost pathetically address you with the solemn adjuration, "Honest Indian?" Whether this phrase is a slur or a compliment to the aborigines of this country, I do not know.

Again, they will agree to a proposal with the appropriate words, "Talk enough when horses fight!" which sentence they will sometimes slightly vary to "Talk enough between gentlemen."

If they wish to borrow anything of you, they will mildly inquire if you have it "about your clothes." As an illustration: a man asked F., the other day, if he had a spare pickax about his clothes. And F. himself gravely inquired of me this evening, at the dinner-table, if I had a *pickle* about my clothes.

If they ask a man an embarrassing question, or in any way have placed him in an equivocal position, they will triumphantly declare that they have "got the dead-wood on him." And they are everlastingly "going nary cent" on those of whose credit they are doubtful. There are many others, which may be common enough everywhere, but as I never happened to hear them before, they have for me all the freshness of originality. You know that it has always been one of my pet rages to trace cant phrases to their origin; but most of those in vogue here would, I verily believe, puzzle Horne Tooke himself.

Letter the Seventh

[The Pioneer, August, 1854]

The NEW LOG-CABIN HOME at INDIAN BAR

SYNOPSIS

Change of residence to Indian Bar. Whether to go to the new camp on muleback over the hill, or on foot by crossing the river. The water-passage decided upon. An escort of Indian Barians. Magnificence of scenery on the way. Gold-miners at work. Their implements. "The color". The Stars and Stripes on a lofty treetop. A camp of tents and cabins. Some of calico shirts and pine boughs. Indian Bar described. Mountains shut out the sun. The "Humbolt" (spelled without the *d* on the sign) the only hotel in the camp. A barroom with a dancing-floor. A cook who plays the violin. A popular place. Clinking glasses and swaggering drinkers. "No place for a lady". The log-cabin residence. Its primitive and makeshift furnishings-The library. No churches, society, etc. "No vegetables but potatoes and onions, no milk, no eggs, no *nothing*."

Letter the Seventh

The New Log-cabin Home at Indian Bar

From our Log Cabin, Indian Bar,

October 7, 1851.

 You will perchance be surprised, dear M., to receive a letter from me dated Indian instead of Rich Bar, but, as many of F.'s most intimate friends reside at this settlement, he concluded to build his log cabin here.

Solemn council was held upon the ways and means of getting "Dame Shirley" to her new home. The general opinion was, that she had better mount her fat mule and ride over the hill, as all agreed that it was very doubtful whether she would be able to cross the logs and jump the rocks which would bar her way by the water-passage. But that obstinate little personage, who has always been haunted with a passionate desire to do everything which people said she could *not* do, made up her willful mind immediately to go by the river. Behold, then, the "Dame" on her winding way, escorted by a deputation of Indian Barians, which had come up for that important purpose.

It is impossible, my sister, for any power of language, over which *I* have command, to convey to you an idea of the wild grandeur and the awful magnificence of the scenery in this vicinity. This fork of the Feather River comes down very much as the water does at Lodore, now gliding along with a liquid measure like a river in a dream, and anon bursting into a thousand glittering foam-beads over the huge rocks, which rise dark, solemn, and weird-like in its midst. The crossings are formed of logs, often moss-grown. Only think how charmingly picturesque to eyes wearied with the costly masonry or carpentry of the bridges at home! At every step gold-diggers, or their operations, greet your vision, sometimes in the form of a dam, sometimes in that of a river turned slightly from its channel to aid the indefatigable gold-hunters in their mining projects. Now, on the side of a hill, you will see a long-tom, a huge machine invented to facilitate the separation of the ore from its native element; or a man busily engaged in working a rocker, a much smaller and simpler machine used for the same object; or, more primitive still, some solitary prospector with a pan of dirt in his hands, which he is carefully washing at the water's edge to see if he can "get the color," as it is technically phrased, which means, literally, the smallest particle of gold.

As we approached Indian Bar the path led several times fearfully near deep holes, from which the laborers were gathering their yellow harvest, and Dame Shirley's small head swam dizzily as she crept shudderingly by.

The first thing which attracted my attention as my new home came in view, was the blended blue, red, and white of the American banner undulating like a many-colored snake amid the lofty verdure of the cedars which garland the brown brow of the hill behind our cabin. This flag was suspended on the Fourth of July last by a patriotic sailor, who climbed to the top of the tree to which he attached it, cutting away the branches as he descended, until it stood among its stately brethren a beautiful moss-wreathed liberty-pole, flinging to the face of heaven the glad colors of the Free.

When I attempt, dear M., to describe one of these spots to you, I regret more than ever the ill health of my childhood, which prevented my attaining any degree of excellence in sketching from nature. Had it not been for that interruption to my artistic education, I might, with a few touches of the pencil or the brush, give you the place and its surroundings. But, alas! my feeble pen will convey to you a very faint idea of its savage beauty.

This Bar is so small that it seems impossible that the tents and cabins scattered over it can amount to a dozen. There are, however, twenty in all, including those formed of calico shirts and pine boughs. With the exception of the paths leading to the different tenements, the entire level is covered with mining-holes, on the edges of which lie the immense piles of dirt and stones which have been removed from the excavations. There is a deep pit in front of our cabin, and another at the side of it, though they are not worked, as, when "prospected," they did not "yield the color."

Not a spot of verdure is to be seen on this place, but the glorious hills rising on every side, vested in foliage of living green, make ample amends for the sterility of the tiny level upon which we camp. The surrounding scenery is infinitely more charming than that of Rich Bar. The river, in hue of a vivid emerald, as if it reflected the hue of the fir-trees above, bordered with a band of dark red, caused by the streams flowing into it from the different sluices, ditches, long-toms, etc., which meander from the hill just back of the Bar, wanders musically along. Across the river, and in front of us, rises nearly perpendicularly a group of mountains, the summits of which are broken into many beautifully cut conical and pyramidal peaks. At the foot and left of these eminences, and a little below our Bar, lies Missouri Bar, which is reached from this spot by a log bridge. Around the latter the river curves in the shape of a crescent, and, singularly enough, the mountain rising behind this bend in the stream outlines itself against the lustrous heaven in a shape as exact and perfect as the moon herself in her first quarter. Within one horn of this crescent the water is a mass of foam-sparkles, and it plays upon the rocks which line its bed an everlasting dirge suggestive of the "grand forever" of the ocean.

At present the sun does not condescend to shine upon Indian Bar at all, and the old settlers tell me that he will not smile upon us for the next three months, but he nestles lovingly in patches of golden glory all along the brows of the different hills around us, and now and then stoops to kiss the topmost wave on the opposite shore of the Río de las Plumas.

The first artificial elegance which attracts your vision is a large rag shanty, roofed, however, with a rude kind of shingles, over the entrance of which is painted, in red capitals, ("to what base uses do we come at last,") the name of the great Humboldt spelt without the *d.* This is the only hotel in this vicinity, and as there is a really excellent bowling-alley attached to it, and the barroom has a floor upon which the miners can dance, and, above all, a cook who can play the violin, it is very popular. But the clinking of glasses, and the swaggering air of some of the drinkers, remind us that it is no place for a lady, so we will pass through the dining-room, and, emerging at the kitchen, in a step or two reach our log cabin. Enter, my dear; you are perfectly welcome. Besides, we could not keep you out if we would, as there is not even a latch on the canvas door, though we really intend, in a day or two, to have a hook put onto it.

The room into which we have just entered is about twenty feet square. It is lined over the top with white cotton cloth, the breadths of which, being sewed together only in spots, stretch gracefully apart in many places, giving one a bird's-eye view of the shingles above. The sides are hung with a gaudy chintz, which I consider a perfect marvel of calico-printing. The artist seems to have exhausted himself on *roses.* From the largest cabbage down to the tiniest Burgundy, he has arranged them in every possible variety of wreath, garland, bouquet, and single flower. They are of all stages of growth, from earliest budhood up to the ravishing beauty of the "last rose of summer." Nor has he confined himself to the colors usually worn by this lovely plant, but, with the daring of a great genius soaring above nature, worshiping the ideal rather than the real, he has painted them brown, purple, green, black, and blue. It would need a floral catalogue to give you the names of *all* the varieties which bloom upon the calico, but, judging by the shapes, which really are much like the originals, I can swear to moss-roses, Burgundies, York and Lancaster, tea-roses, and multifloras.

A curtain of the above-described chintz (I shall hem it at the first opportunity) divides off a portion of the room, behind which stands a bedstead that in ponderosity leaves the Empire couches far behind. But before I attempt the furniture let me finish describing the cabin itself.

The fireplace is built of stones and mud, the chimney finished off with alternate layers of rough sticks and this same rude mortar. Contrary to the usual custom, it is built inside, as it was thought that arrangement would make the room more comfortable, and you may imagine the queer appearance of this unfinished pile of stones, mud, and sticks. The mantelpiece (remember that on this portion of a great building some artists, by their exquisite workmanship, have become world-renowned) is formed of a beam of wood covered with strips of tin procured from cans, upon which still remain, in black hieroglyphics, the names of the different eatables which they formerly contained. Two smooth stones (how delightfully primitive!) do duty as fire-dogs. I suppose that it would be no more than civil to call a hole two feet square, in one side of the room, a window, although it is as yet guiltless of glass. F. tried to coax the proprietor of the Empire to let him have a window from that pine-and-canvas palace, but he, of course, declined, as to part with it would really inconvenience himself. So F. has sent to Marysville for some glass, though it is the general opinion that the snow will render the trail impassible for mules before we can get it. In this case we shall tack up a piece of cotton cloth, and should it chance at any time to be very cold, hang a blanket before the opening. At present the weather is so mild that it is pleasanter as it is, though we have a fire in the mornings and evenings, more, however, for luxury than because we really need it. For my part, I almost hope that we shall not be able to get any glass, for you will perhaps remember that it was a pet habit of mine, in my own room, to sit by a great fire, in the depth of winter, with my window open.

One of our friends had nailed up an immense quantity of unhemmed cotton cloth—very coarse—in front of this opening, and as he evidently prided himself upon the elegant style in which he had arranged the drapery, it went to my heart to take it down and suspend in its place some pretty blue linen curtains which I had brought from the valley. My toilet-table is formed of a trunk elevated upon two claret-cases, and by draping it with some more of the blue linen neatly fringed, it really will look quite handsome, and when I have placed upon it my rosewood workbox, a large cushion of crimson brocade, some Chinese ornaments of exquisitely carved ivory, and two or three Bohemian-glass cologne-stands, it would not disgrace a lady's chamber at home.

The looking-glass is one of those which come in paper cases for dolls' houses. How different from the full-length psyches so almost indispensable to a dressing-room in the States!

The wash-stand is another trunk, covered with a towel, upon which you will see, for bowl, a large vegetable-dish, for ewer, a common-sized dining-pitcher. Near this, upon a small cask, is placed a pail, which is daily filled with water from the river. I brought with me from Marysville a handsome carpet, a hair mattress, pillows, a profusion of bed-linen, quilts, blankets, towels, etc., so that, in spite of the oddity of most of my furniture, I am, in reality, as thoroughly comfortable here as I could be in the most elegant palace.

We have four chairs, which were brought from the Empire. I seriously proposed having three-legged stools. With my usual desire for symmetry, I thought that they would be more in keeping; but as I was told that it would be a great deal of trouble to get them made, I was fain to put up with mere chairs. So you see that even in the land of gold itself one cannot have everything that she desires. An ingenious individual in the neighborhood, blessed with a large bump for mechanics, and good nature, made me a sort of wide bench, which, covered with a neat plaid, looks quite sofa-like. A little pine table, with oilcloth tacked over the top of it, stands in one corner of the room, upon which are arranged the chess and cribbage boards. There is a larger one for dining purposes, and as unpainted pine has always a most dreary look, F. went everywhere in search of oilcloth for it, but there was none at any of the bars. At last, "Ned," the Humboldt Paganini, remembered two old monte-table covers which had been thrown aside as useless. I received them thankfully, and, with my planning and Ned's mechanical genius, we patched up quite a respectable covering. To be sure, the ragged condition of the primitive material compelled us to have at one end an extra border, but that only agreeably relieved the monotony. I must mention that the floor is so uneven that no article of furniture gifted with four legs pretends to stand upon but three at once, so that the chairs, tables, etc., remind you constantly of a dog with a sore foot.

At each end of the mantelpiece is arranged a candlestick, not, much to my regret, a block of wood with a hole in the center of it, but a real britanniaware candlestick. The space between is gayly ornamented with F.'s meerschaum, several styles of clay pipes, cigars, cigarritos, and every procurable variety of tobacco, for, you know, the aforesaid individual is a perfect devotee of the Indian weed. If I should give you a month of Sundays, you would never guess what we use in lieu of a bookcase, so I will put you out of your misery by informing you instantly that it is nothing more nor less than a candle-box which contains the library, consisting of a Bible and prayer-book, Shakespeare, Spenser, Coleridge, Shelley, Keats, Lowell's Fable for Critics, Walton's Complete Angler, and some Spanish books,— spiritual instead of material lights, you see.

There, my dainty Lady Molly, I have given you, I fear, a wearisomely minute description of my new home. How would you like to winter in such an abode? in a place where there are no newspapers, no churches, lectures, concerts, or theaters; no fresh books; no shopping, calling, nor gossiping little tea-drinkings; no parties, no balls, no picnics, no tableaus, no charades, no latest fashions, no daily mail (we have an express once a month), no promenades, no rides or drives; no vegetables but potatoes and onions, no milk, no eggs, no *nothing*? Now, I expect to be very happy here. This strange, odd life fascinates me. As for churches, "the groves were God's first temples," "and for the strength of the hills, the Swiss mountains bless him"; and as to books, I read Shakespeare, David, Spenser, Paul, Coleridge, Burns, and Shelley, which are never old. In good sooth, I fancy that nature intended me for an Arab or some other nomadic barbarian, and by mistake my soul got packed up in a Christianized set of bones and muscles. How I shall ever be able to content myself to live in a decent, proper, well-behaved house, where toilet-tables are toilet-tables, and not an ingenious combination of trunk and claret-cases, where lanterns are not broken bottles, bookcases not candle-boxes, and trunks not wash-stands, but every article of furniture, instead of being a makeshift, is its own useful and elegantly finished self, I am sure I do not know. However, when too much appalled at the humdrummish prospect, I console myself with the beautiful promises, that "sufficient unto the day is the evil thereof," and "as thy days, so shall thy strength be," and trust that when it is again my lot to live amid the refinements and luxuries of civilization, I shall endure them with becoming philosophy and fortitude.

Letter the Eighth

[The Pioneer, September, 1854]

LIFE and CHARACTERS at INDIAN BAR

SYNOPSIS

Ned, the mulatto cook and the Paganini of the Humboldt Hotel. A naval character. His ecstasy upon hearing of the coming of the author to the Bar. Suggestion of a strait-jacket for him. "The only petticoated astonishment on this Bar". First dinner at the log cabin. Ned's pretentious setting of the pine dining-table. The Bar ransacked for viands. The bill of fare. Ned an accomplished violinist. "Chock," his white accompanist. The author serenaded. An unappreciated "artistic" gift. A guide of the Frémont expedition camps at Indian Bar. A linguist, and former chief of the Crow Indians. Cold-blooded recitals of Indian fights. Indians near the Bar expected to make a murderous attack upon the miners. The guide's council with them. Flowery reply of the Indians. A studious Quaker. His merciless frankness and regard for truth. "The Squire," and how he was elected justice of the peace. Miners prefer to rule themselves.

Letter the Eighth
Life and Characters at Indian Bar
From our Log Cabin, Indian Bar,
October 20, 1851.

Having seen me, dear M., safely enthroned in my beautiful log palace with its outer walls all tapestried with moss, perhaps you would like a description of the coronation-dinner!

You must know that "Ned," the Paganini of the Humboldt, (who, by the way, is almost an historic, or, better perhaps, naval, character, inasmuch as he was *cook* on board of the Somers when her captain performed his little tragedy, to the horror of an entire nation,) had been in such a state of ecstasy ever since he had heard of the promised advent of Mrs. ——, that his *proprietors*, as Ned grandly calls them, had serious fears of being compelled to strait-jacket him.

"You see, sir," said Ned, "when the queen" (with Ned, as with the rest of the world, "a substitute shines brightly as a queen until a queen be by,"—and I am the only petticoated astonishment on this Bar) "arrives, *she* will appreciate my culinary efforts. It is really discouraging, sir, after I have exhausted my skill in preparing a dish, to see the gentlemen devour it with as much unconcern as though it had been cooked by a mere bungler in our art"!

When we entered our new home, we found the cloth—it was a piece left of that which lined the room overhead—already laid. As it was unhemmed and somewhat tattered at the ends, an imaginative mind might fancy it fringed on purpose, though, like the poor little Marchioness with her orange-peel and water, one would have to *make believe* very hard. Unfortunately, it was not wide enough for the table, and a dashing border of white pine banded each side of it. Ned had invested an unknown quantity of gold-dust in a yard of diaper,—awfully coarse,—which, divided into four pieces, and fringed to match the tablecloth, he had placed napkin-wise in the tumblers. He had evidently ransacked the whole bar to get viands wherewith to decorate the various dishes, which were as follows.

First Course
OYSTER SOUP

Second Course
FRIED SALMON CAUGHT FROM THE RIVER

Third Course
ROAST BEEF & BOILED HAM

Fourth Course
FRIED OYSTERS

Vegetables
POTATOES & ONIONS

Pastry
MINCE PIE, & PUDDING MADE WITHOUT EGGS OR MILK

Dessert
MADEIRA NUTS & RAISINS

Wines
CLARET & CHAMPAGNE

Coffee

I found that Ned had not overrated his powers. The dinner, when one considers the materials of which it was composed, was really excellent. The soup was truly a great work of art; the fried oysters dreamily delicious; and as to the coffee, Ned must have got the receipt for making it from the very angel who gave the beverage to Mahomet to restore that individual's decayed moisture.

Ned himself waited, dressed in a brand-new flannel shirt and calico ditto, his hair—he is a light mulatto—frizzled to the most intense degree of corkscrewity, and a benign and self-satisfied smile irradiating his face, such as *should* illumine the features of a great artist when he knows that he has achieved something, the memory of which the world will not willingly let die. In truth, he needed but white kid gloves to have been worthy of standing behind the chair of Count d'Orsay himself. So grand was his air, so ceremonious his every motion, that we forgot we were living in the heart of the Sierra Nevada; forgot that our home was a log cabin of mere primitive rudeness; forgot that we were sitting at a rough pine table covered with a ragged piece of four-cent cotton cloth, eating soup with iron spoons!

I wish, my funny little Molly, that you could have been here clairvoyantly. It was one of those scenes, just touched with that fine and almost imperceptible *perfume* of the ludicrous, in which you especially delight. There are a thousand minute shreds of the absurd which my duller sense overlooks, but which never can hope to escape your mirth-loving vision.

Ned really plays beautifully on the violin. There is a white man, by the name of "Chock," who generally accompanies him. Of course, true daughter of Eve that you are, you will wish to know "right off" what Chock's *other* name is. Young woman, I am ashamed of you! Who ever asks for the *other* name of Alexander, of Hannibal, of Homer? Suffice it that he is Chock by himself,—Chock, and assistant violinist to Paganini Vattal Ned.

Ned and one of his musical cronies—a white man—gave me a serenade the other evening. As it was quite cold, F. made them come inside the cabin. It was the richest thing possible, to see the patronizing and yet serene manner with which Ned directed his companion what marches, preludes, etc., to play for the amusement of that profound culinary and musical critic, Dame Shirley.

It must be confessed that Ned's love of the beautiful is not quite so correct as his taste in cooking and violin-playing. This morning a gentle knock at my door was followed by that polite person, bearing in triumph a small waiter, purloined from the Humboldt, on which stood in state, festooned with tumblers, a gaudy pitcher, which would have thrown Tearsoul and Lelie into ecstasies of delight. It was almost as wonderful a specimen of art as my chintz hanging. The groundwork is pure white, upon which, in bas-relief, are *executed* two diabolical-looking bandits, appallingly bewhiskered and mustached, dressed in red coats, yellow pantaloons, green boots, orange-colored caps with brown feathers in them, and sky-blue bows and arrows. Each of the fascinating vagabonds is attended by a bird-of-paradise-colored dog, with a crimson tail waggingly depicted. They are embowered beneath a morning-glory vine, evidently a species of the Convolvulus unknown in America, as each one of its pink leaves, springing from purple stems, is three times the size of the bandit's head.

Ned could not have admired it more if it had been a jar of richest porcelain or a rare Etruscan vase, and when I gently suggested that it was a pity to rob the barroom of so elegant an ornament, he answered, "Miners can't appreciate a handsome pitcher, any more than they can good cooking, and Mrs. —— will please to keep it."

Alas! I would infinitely have preferred the humblest brown jug, for that really *has* a certain beauty of its own, and, besides, it would have been in keeping with my cabin. However, that good creature looked upon the miraculous vegetable, the fabulous quadrupeds, and the impossible bipeds, with so much pride that I had not the heart to tell him that the pitcher was a fright, but, graciously accepting it, I hid it out of sight as quickly as possible, on the trunk wash-stand behind the curtain.

We breakfast at nine and dine at six, with a dish of soup at noon for luncheon. Do not think we fare as sumptuously *every* day as we did at the coronation-dinner. By no means; and it is said that there will probably be many weeks, during the season, when we shall have neither onions, potatoes, nor fresh meat. It is feared that the former will not keep through the whole winter, and the rancheros cannot at all times drive in cattle for butchering, on account of the expected snow.

Ned is not the only distinguished person residing on this Bar. There is a man camping here who was one of Colonel Frémont's guides during his travels through California. He is fifty years of age perhaps, and speaks several languages to perfection. As he has been a wanderer for many years, and for a long time was the principal chief of the Crow Indians, his adventures are extremely interesting. He chills the blood of the green young miners, who, unacquainted with the arts of war and subjugation, congregate around him by the cold-blooded manner in which he relates the Indian fights that he has been engaged in.

There is quite a band of this wild people herding a few miles below us, and soon after my arrival it was confidently affirmed and believed by many that they were about to make a murderous attack upon the miners. This man, who can make himself understood in almost any language, and has a great deal of influence over all Indians, went to see them, and told them that such an attempt would result in their own certain destruction. They said that they had never thought of such a thing; that the Americans were like the grass in the valleys, and the Indians fewer than the flowers of the Sierra Nevada.

Among other oddities, there is a person here who is a rabid admirer of Lippard. I have heard him gravely affirm that Lippard was the greatest author the world ever saw, and that if one of his novels and the most fascinating work of ancient or modern times lay side by side, he would choose the former, even though he had already repeatedly perused it. He *studies* Lippard just as other folks do Shakespeare, and yet the man has read and *admires* the majestic prose of Chilton, and is quite familiar with the best English classics! He is a Quaker, and his merciless and unmitigated regard for truth is comically grand, and nothing amuses me more than to draw out that peculiar characteristic. For instance, after talking *at* him the most beautiful and eloquent things that I can think of, I will pitilessly nail him in this wise:—

"Now, I know that *you* agree with me, Mr. ——?"

It is the richest and broadest farce in this flattering and deceitful world to see him look right into my eyes while he answers smilingly, without the least evasion or reserve, the astounding *truth*,—

"I have not heard a word that you have been saying for the last half-hour; I have been thinking of something else!"

His dreamland reveries on these occasions are supposed to be a profound meditation upon the character and writings of his pet author. I am always glad to have him visit us, as some one of us is sure to be most unflatteringly electrified by his uncompromising veracity. I am, myself, generally the victim, as I make it a point to give him every opportunity for the display of this unusual peculiarity. Not but that I have had disagreeable truth told me often enough, but heretofore people have done it out of spitefulness; but Mr. ——, who is the kindest-hearted of mortals, never dreams that his merciless frankness can possibly wound one's self-love.

But *the* great man—officially considered—of the entire river is the "Squire," as he is jestingly called. It had been rumored for some time that we were about to become a law-and-order-loving community, and when I requested an explanation, I was informed that a man had gone all the way to Hamilton, the county seat, to get himself made into a justice of the peace. Many shook their wise heads, and doubted, even if suited to the situation, which they say he is not, whether he would *take* here; and certain rebel spirits affirmed that he would be invited to *walk over the hill* before he had been in the community twenty-four hours, which is a polite way these free-and-easy young people have of turning out of town an obnoxious individual. Not that the Squire is particularly objectionable *per se,* but in virtue of his office, and his supposed ineligibility to fill the same. Besides, the people here wish to have the fun of ruling themselves. Miners are as fond of playing at law making and dispensing as French novelists are of "playing at Providence." They say, also, that he was not elected by the voice of the people, but that his personal friends nominated and voted for him unknown to the rest of the community. This is perhaps true. At least, I have heard some of the most respectable men here observe that had they been aware of the Squire's name being up as candidate for an office which, though insignificant elsewhere, is one of great responsibility in a mining community, they should certainly have gone against his election.

Last night I had the honor of an introduction to "*His* Honor." Imagine a middle-sized man, quite stout, with a head disproportionately large, crowned with one of those immense foreheads eked out with a slight baldness (wonder if, according to the flattering popular superstition, he has *thought* his hair off) which enchant phrenologists, but which one *never* sees brooding above the soulful orbs of the great ones of the earth; a smooth, fat face, gray eyes, and prominent chin, the *tout ensemble* characterized by an expression of the utmost meekness and gentleness, which expression contrasts rather funnily with a satanic goatee,—and you have our good Squire.

You know, M., that it takes the same *kind* of power—differing, of course, in degree—to govern twenty men that it does to rule a million; and although the Squire is sufficiently intelligent, and the kindest-hearted creature in the world, he evidently does *not* possess that peculiar tact, talent, gift, or whatever it is called, which makes Napoleons, Mahomets, and Cromwells, and which is absolutely necessary to keep in order such a strangely amalgamated community, representing as it does the four quarters of the globe, as congregates upon this river.

However, I suppose that we must take the goods the gods provide, satisfied that if our King Log does no good, he is too sincerely desirous of fulfilling his duty to do any harm. But I really feel sorry for this mere young Daniel come to judgment when I think of the gauntlet which the wicked wits will make him run when he tries his first cause.

However, the Squire may, after all, succeed. As yet he has had no opportunity of making use of his credentials in putting down miners' law, which is, of course, the famous code of Judge Lynch. In the mean time we all sincerely pray that he may be successful in his laudable undertaking, for justice in the hands of a mob, however respectable, is, at best, a fearful thing.

Letter the Ninth
[The Pioneer, October, 1854]
THEFT of GOLD-DUST—TRIAL and PUNISHMENT
SYNOPSIS

The "Squire's" first opportunity to exercise his judicial power. Holding court in a barroom. The jury "treated" by the Squire. Theft of gold-dust, and arrest of suspect. A miners' meeting. Fear that they would hang the prisoner. Regular trial decided upon, at the Empire, Rich Bar, where the gold-dust was stolen. A suggestion of thrift. Landlords to profit by trial, wherever held. Mock respect of the miners for the Squire. Elect a president at the trial. The Squire allowed to play at judge. Lay counsel for prosecution and defense. Ingenious defense of the accused. Verdict of guilty. Light sentence, on account of previous popularity and inoffensive conduct. Thirty-nine lashes, and to leave the river. Owner of gold-dust indemnified by transfer of thief's interest in a mine. A visit to Smith's Bar. Crossing the river on log bridges. Missouri Bar. Smith's a sunny camp, unlike Indian. Frenchman's Bar, another sunny spot. "Yank," the owner of a log-cabin store. Shrewdness and simplicity. Hopeless ambition to be "cute and smart". The "Indiana girl" impossible to Yank. "A superior and splendid woman, but no polish". Yank's "olla podrida of heterogeneous merchandise". The author meets the banished gold-dust thief. Subscription by the miners on his banishment. A fool's errand to establish his innocence. An oyster-supper bet. The thief's statements totally incompatible with innocence.

Letter the Ninth

Theft of Gold-Dust—Trial and Punishment

From our Log Cabin, Indian Bar,

October 29, 1851.

Well, my dear M., our grand Squire, whom I sketched for you in my last letter, has at length had an opportunity to exercise (or rather to *try* to do so) his judicial power upon a criminal case. His first appearance as justice of the peace took place a week ago, and was caused, I think, by a prosecution for debt. On that momentous occasion, the proceeding having been carried on in the barroom of the Empire, it is said that our young Daniel stopped the court twice in order to treat the jury!

But let me tell you about the trial which has just taken place. On Sunday evening last, Ned Paganini, rushing wildly up to our cabin, and with eyes so enormously dilated that they absolutely looked *all* white, exclaimed that "Little John" had been arrested for stealing four hundred dollars from the proprietor of the Empire, and that he was at that very moment undergoing an examination before the Squire in the barroom of the Humboldt, where he was apprehended while betting at monte. "And," added Ned, with a most awe-inspiring shake of his corkscrews, "there is no doubt but that he will be hung!"

Of course I was inexpressibly shocked at Ned's news, for Little John, as he is always called (who, by the way, is about the last person, as every one remarked, that would have been suspected), seemed quite like an acquaintance, as he was waiter at the Empire when I boarded there. I hurried F. off as quickly as possible to inquire into the truth of the report. He soon returned with the following particulars.

It seems that Mr. B., who on Sunday morning wished to pay a bill, on taking his purse from between the two mattresses of the bed whereon he was accustomed to sleep, which stood in the common sitting-room of the family, found that four hundred dollars in gold-dust was missing. He did not for one moment suspect Little John, in whom himself and wife had always placed the utmost confidence, until a man, who happened to be in the barroom towards evening, mentioned casually that Little John was then at the Humboldt betting, or, to speak technically, "bucking" away large sums at monte. Mr. B., who knew that he had no money of his own, immediately came over to Indian Bar and had him arrested on suspicion. Although he had lost several ounces, he had still about a hundred dollars remaining. But as it is impossible to identify gold-dust, Mr. B. could not swear that the money was his.

Of course the prisoner loudly protested his innocence, and as he was very drunk, the Squire adjourned all further proceedings until the next day, placing him under keepers for the night.

On the following morning I was awakened very early by a tremendous "Aye," so deep and mighty that it almost seemed to shake the cabin with its thrilling emphasis. I sprang up and ran to the window, but could *see* nothing, of course, as our house stands behind the Humboldt, but I could easily understand, from the confused murmur of many voices and the rapidly succeeding "ayes" and "noes," that a large crowd had collected in front of the latter. My first apprehension was expressed by my bursting into tears and exclaiming,—

"Oh! F., for God's sake, rise; the mob are going to hang Little John!"

And my fear was not so absurd as you might at first imagine, for men have often been executed in the mines for stealing a much smaller sum than four hundred dollars.

F. went to the Humboldt, and returned in a few minutes to tell me that I might stop weeping, for John was going to have a regular trial. The crowd was merely a miners' meeting, called by Mr. B. for the purpose of having the trial held at the Empire for the convenience of his wife, who could not walk over to Indian Bar to give her evidence in the case. However, as her deposition could easily have been taken, malicious people *will* say that it was for the convenience of her husband's *pockets*, as it was well known that at whichever house the trial took place the owner thereof would make a handsome profit from the sale of dinners, drinks, etc., to the large number of people who would congregate to witness the proceedings. Miners are proverbial for their reverence for the sex. Of course everything ought to yield where a lady is concerned, and they all very properly agreed, *nem. con.*, to Mr. B.'s request.

The Squire consented to hold the court at Rich Bar, although many think that thereby he compromised his judicial dignity, as his office is on Indian Bar. I must confess I see not how he could have done otherwise. The miners were only too ready, so much do they object to a justice of the peace, to take the case *entirely* out of his hands if their wishes were not complied with, which, to confess the truth, they *did*, even after all his concessions, though they *pretended* to keep up a sort of mock respect for his office.

Everybody went to Rich Bar. No one remained to protect the calico shanties, the rag huts, and the log cabins, from the much talked of Indian attack—but your humble servant and Paganini Ned.

When the people, the mighty people, had assembled at the Empire, they commenced proceedings by voting in a president and jury of their own, though they kindly consented (how very condescending!) that the Squire might *play at judge* by sitting at the side of *their* elected magistrate! This honor the Squire seemed to take as a sort of salve to his wounded dignity, and with unprecedented meekness *accepted* it. A young Irishman from St. Louis was appointed counsel for John, and a Dr. C. acted for the prosecution. Neither of them, however, was a lawyer.

The evidence against the prisoner was, that he had no money previously, that he had slept at the Empire a night or two before, and that he knew where Mr. B. was in the habit of keeping his gold-dust, with a few other circumstances equally unimportant. His only defense was, of course, to account for the money, which he tried to do by the following ingenious story.

He said that his father, who resides at Stockholm,—he is a Swede,—had sent him, two months previously, five hundred dollars through the express, which had been brought to him from San Francisco by a young man whose name is Miller; that he told no one of the circumstance, but buried the money (a common habit with the miner) on the summit of a hill about half a mile from Indian Bar; that, being intoxicated on Sunday morning, he had dug it up for the purpose of gambling with it; and that Mr. M., who had gone to Marysville a week before, and would return in a fortnight, could confirm his story. When asked if he had received a letter with the money, he replied that he did, but, having placed it between the lining and the top of his cap, he had unfortunately lost it. He earnestly affirmed his innocence, and, through his counsel, entreated the court, should he be condemned, to defer the execution of his sentence until the arrival of Miller, by whom he could prove all that he had stated. Notwithstanding the florid eloquence of W., the jury brought in a verdict of guilty, and condemned him to receive thirty-nine lashes at nine o'clock the following morning, and to leave the river, never to return to it, within twenty-four hours; a claim, of which he owned a part, to be made over to Mr. B. to indemnify him for his loss. His punishment was very light, on account of his previous popularity and inoffensive conduct. In spite of his really ingenious defense, no one has the least doubt of his guilt but his lawyer and the Squire. They as firmly believe him an innocent and much-injured man.

Yesterday morning I made my visit to Smith's Bar. In order to reach it, it was necessary to cross the river, on a bridge formed of two logs, to Missouri Bar. This flat, which has been worked but very little, has a path leading across it, a quarter of a mile in length. It contains but two or three huts, no very extensive diggings having as yet been discovered upon it. About in the middle of it, and close to the side of the trail, is situated a burial-spot, where not only its dead repose, but those who die on Indian Bar are also brought for interment. On arriving at the termination of the level, another log bridge leads to Smith's Bar, which, although it lies upon the same side of the river as our settlement, is seldom approached, as I before observed, except by crossing to Missouri Bar and back again from that to Smith's. The hills rise so perpendicularly between this latter and Indian Bar that it is utterly impossible for a woman to follow on the trail along their side, and it is no child's-play for even the most hardy mountaineer to do it.

This level (Smith's Bar) is large and quite thickly settled. More gold has been taken from it than from any other settlement on the river. Although the scenery here is not so strikingly picturesque as that surrounding my new home, it is perhaps infinitely more lovely, and certainly more desirable as a place of residence, than the latter, because the sun shines upon it all winter, and we can take long walks about it in many directions. Now, Indian Bar is so completely covered with excavations and tenements that it is utterly impossible to promenade upon it at all. Whenever I wish for exercise, I am *compelled* to cross the river, which, of course, I cannot do without company, and as the latter is not always procurable (F.'s profession calling him much from home), I am obliged to stay indoors more than I like, or is conducive to my health.

A short but steep ascent from Smith's Bar leads you to another bench, as miners call it, almost as large as itself, which is covered with trees and grass, and is a most lovely place. From here one has a charming view of a tiny bar called Frenchman's. It is a most sunny little spot, covered with the freshest greensward, and nestling lovingly, like a petted darling, in the embracing curve of a crescent-shaped hill opposite. It looks more like some sheltered nook amid the blue mountains of New England than anything I have ever yet seen in California. Formerly there was a deer-lick upon it, and I am told that on every dewy morning or starlit evening you might see a herd of pretty creatures gathering in antlered beauty about its margin. Now, however, they are seldom met with, the advent of gold-hunting humanity having driven them far up into the hills.

The man who keeps the store at which we stopped (a log cabin without any floor) goes by the sobriquet of "Yank," and is quite a character in his way. He used to be a peddler in the States, and is remarkable for an intense ambition to be thought what the Yankees call "cute and smart,"—an ambition which his true and good heart will never permit him to achieve. He is a great friend of mine (I am always interested in that bizarre mixture of shrewdness and simplicity of which he is a distinguished specimen), and takes me largely into his confidence as to the various ways he has of *doing* green miners,— all the merest delusion on his part, you understand, for he is the most honest of God's creatures, and would not, I verily believe, cheat a man out of a grain of golden sand to save his own harmless and inoffensive life. He is popularly supposed to be smitten with the charms of the "Indiana girl," but I confess I doubt it, for Yank himself informed me, confidentially, that, "though a very superior and splendid woman, she had no *polish*"!

He is an indefatigable "snapper-up of unconsidered trifles," and his store is the most comical olla podrida of heterogeneous merchandise that I ever saw. There is nothing you can ask for but what he has,— from crowbars down to cambric-needles; from velveteen trousers up to broadcloth coats of the jauntiest description. The *quality* of his goods, it must be confessed, is sometimes rather equivocal. His collection of novels is by far the largest, the greasiest, and the "yellowest-kivered" of any to be found on the river. I will give you an instance of the variety of his possessions.

I wanted some sealing-wax to mend a broken chess-piece, having by some strange carelessness left the box containing mine in Marysville. I inquired everywhere for it, but always got laughed at for supposing that any one would be so absurd as to bring such an article into the mountains. As a forlorn hope, I applied to Yank. Of course he had plenty! The best of it is, that, whenever he produces any of these out-of-the-way things, he always says that he brought them from the States, which proves that he had a remarkable degree of foresight when he left his home three years ago.

While I sat chatting with Yank I heard some one singing loudly, and apparently very gayly, a negro melody, and, the next moment, who should enter but Little John, who had been whipped, according to sentence, three hours previously. As soon as he saw me he burst into tears, and exclaimed,—

"Oh! Mrs. ——, a heartless mob has beaten me cruelly, has taken all my money from me, and has decreed that I, who am an innocent man, should leave the mountains without a cent of money to assist me on my way!"

The latter part of his speech, as I afterwards discovered, was *certainly* a lie, for he knew that a sum amply sufficient to pay his expenses to Marysville had been subscribed by the very people who believed him guilty. Of course his complaints were extremely painful to me. You know how weakly pitiful I always am towards wicked people; for it seems to me that they are so much more to be compassionated than the good.

But what *could* I say to poor John? I did not for one moment doubt his entire guilt, and so, as people often do on such occasions, I took refuge in a platitude.

"Well, John," I sagely remarked, "I hope that you did not take the money. And only think how much happier you are in that case, than if you had been beaten and abused as you say you have, and at the same time were a criminal!"

I must confess, much as it tells against my eloquence, that John did not receive my well-meant attempt at consolation with that pious gratitude which such an injured innocent ought to have exhibited, but, F. luckily calling me at that moment, I was spared any more of his tearful complaints.

Soon after our return to the cabin, John's lawyer and the Squire called upon us. They declared their perfect conviction of his innocence, and the latter remarked that if any one would accompany him he would walk up to the spot and examine the hole from whence the culprit affirmed that he had taken his money only three days ago, as he very naturally supposed that it would still exhibit signs of having been recently opened. It was finally agreed that the victim, who had never described the place to the Squire, should give a minute description of it, unheard by His Honor, to F., and afterwards should lead the former, accompanied by his counsel, (no one else could be persuaded to make such martyrs of themselves,) to the much-talked-of spot. And, will you believe it, M.? those two obstinate men actually persevered, although it was nearly dark, and a very cold, raw, windy night, in walking half a mile up one of the steepest hills on what the rest thought a perfect fool's errand! To be sure, they have triumphed for the moment, for the Squire's description, on their return, tallied exactly with that previously given to F. But, alas! the infidels remained infidels still.

Then W. bet an oyster-supper for the whole party, which F. took up, that Miller, on his return, would confirm his client's statement. For fear of accidents, we had the oysters that night, and very nice they were, I assure you. This morning the hero of the last three days vanished to parts unknown. And thus endeth the Squire's first attempt to sit in judgment in a criminal case. I regret his failure very much, as do many others. Whether any one else could have succeeded better, I cannot say. But I am sure that no person could more sincerely *desire* and *try* to act for the best good of the community than the Squire.

I suppose that I should be as firm a believer in John's innocence as any one, had he not said to F. and others that if he had taken the money they could not *prove* it against him, and many other similar things, which seem to me totally incompatible with innocence.

Letter the Tenth

[The Pioneer, November, 1854]

AMATEUR MINING—HAIRBREADTH 'SCAPES, &C.

SYNOPSIS

Three dollars and twenty-five cents in gold-dust. Sorry she learned the trade. The resulting losses and suffering. Secret of the brilliant successes of former gold-washeresses. Salting the ground by miners in order to deceive their fair visitors. Erroneous ideas of richness of auriferous dirt resulting therefrom. Rarity of lucky strikes. Claim yielding ten dollars a day considered valuable. Consternation and near-disaster in the author's cabin. Trunk of forest giant rolls down hill. Force broken by rock near cabin. Terror of careless woodman. Another narrow escape at Smith's Bar. Pursuit and escape of woodman. Two sudden deaths at Indian Bar. Inquest in the open. Cosmopolitan gathering thereat. Wife of one of the deceased an advanced bloomer. Animadversions on strong-minded bloomers seeking their rights. California pheasant, gallina del campo of the Spaniards. Pines and dies in captivity. Smart, harmless earthquake-shocks.

Letter the Tenth
Amateur Mining-Hairbreadth 'Scapes, &c.
From our Log Cabin, Indian Bar,
November 25, 1851.

Nothing of importance has happened since I last wrote you, except that I have become a *mineress*, that is, if the having washed a pan of dirt with my own hands, and procured therefrom three dollars and twenty-five cents in gold-dust, which I shall inclose in this letter, will entitle me to the name. I can truly say, with the blacksmith's apprentice at the close of his first day's work at the anvil, that I am sorry I learned the trade, for I wet my feet, tore my dress, spoilt a pair of new gloves, nearly froze my fingers, got an awful headache, took cold, and lost a valuable breastpin, in this my labor of love. After such melancholy self-sacrifice on my part, I trust you will duly prize my gift. I can assure you that it is the last golden handiwork you will ever receive from Dame Shirley.

Apropos of lady gold-washers in general, it is a common habit with people residing in towns in the vicinity of the diggings to make up pleasure-parties to those places. Each woman of the company will exhibit, on her return, at least twenty dollars of the oro, which she will gravely inform you she has just panned out from a single basinful of the soil. This, of course, gives strangers a very erroneous idea of the average richness of auriferous dirt. I myself thought (now, don't laugh) that one had but to saunter gracefully along romantic streamlets on sunny afternoons, with a parasol and white kid gloves perhaps, and to stop now and then to admire the scenery, and carelessly rinse out a small panful of yellow sand (without detriment to the white kids, however, so easy did I fancy the whole process to be), in order to fill one's work-bag with the most beautiful and rare specimens of the precious mineral. Since I have been here I have discovered my mistake, and also the secret of the brilliant success of former gold-washeresses.

The miners are in the habit of flattering the vanity of their fair visitors by scattering a handful of "salt" (which, strange to say, is *exactly* the color of gold-dust, and has the remarkable property of often bringing to light very curious lumps of the ore) through the dirt before the dainty fingers touch it, and the dear creatures go home with their treasures, firmly believing that mining is the prettiest pastime in the world.

I had no idea of permitting such a costly joke to be played upon me; so I said but little of my desire to "go through the motions" of gold-washing, until one day, when, as I passed a deep hole in which several men were at work, my companion requested the owner to fill a small pan, which I had in my hand, with dirt from the bed-rock. This request was, of course, granted, and the treasure having been conveyed to the edge of the river, I succeeded, after much awkward maneuvering on my own part, and considerable assistance from friend H., an experienced miner, in gathering together the above-specified sum. All the diggers of our acquaintance say that it is an excellent "prospect," even to come from the bed-rock, where, naturally, the richest dirt is found.

To be sure, there are, now and then, "lucky strikes," such, for instance, as that mentioned in a former letter, where a person took out of a single basinful of soil two hundred and fifty-six dollars. But such luck is as rare as the winning of a hundred-thousand-dollar prize in a lottery. We are acquainted with many here whose gains have *never* amounted to much more than wages, that is, from six to eight dollars a day. And a claim which yields a man a steady income of ten dollars *per diem* is considered as very valuable.

I received an immense fright the other morning. I was sitting by the fire, quietly reading "Lewis Arundel," which had just fallen into my hands, when a great shout and trampling of feet outside attracted my attention. Naturally enough, my first impulse was to run to the door, but scarcely had I risen to my feet for that purpose, when a mighty crash against the side of the cabin, shaking it to the foundation, threw me suddenly upon my knees. So violent was the shock that for a moment I thought the staunch old logs, mossed with the pale verdure of ages, were falling in confusion around me.

As soon as I could collect my scattered senses, I looked about to see what had happened. Several stones had fallen from the back of the chimney, mortar from the latter covered the hearth, the cloth overhead was twisted into the funniest possible wrinkles, the couch had jumped two feet from the side of the house, the little table lay on its back, holding up *four* legs instead of *one*, the chessmen were rolling merrily about in every direction, the dishes had all left their usual places, the door, which, ever since, has obstinately refused to let itself be shut, was thrown violently open, while an odd-looking pile of articles lay in the middle of the room, which, upon investigation, was found to consist of a pail, a broom, a bell, some candlesticks, a pack of cards, a loaf of bread, a pair of boots, a bunch of cigars, and some clay pipes (the only things, by the way, rendered utterly *hors de combat* in the assault). But one piece of furniture retained its attitude, and that was the elephantine bedstead, which nothing short of an earthquake could move. Almost at the same moment several acquaintances rushed in, begging me not to be alarmed, as the danger was past.

"But what has happened?" I eagerly inquired.

"O, a large tree, which was felled this morning, has rolled down from the brow of the hill." And its having struck a rock a few feet from the house, losing thereby the most of its force, had alone saved us from utter destruction.

I grew sick with terror when I understood the awful fate from which Providence had preserved me, and even now my heart leaps painfully with mingled fear and gratitude when I think how closely that pale death-shadow glided by me, and of the loving care which forbade it to linger upon our threshold.

Every one who saw the forest giant descending the hill with the force of a mighty torrent expected to see the cabin instantly prostrated to the earth. As it was, they all say that it swayed from the perpendicular more than six inches.

Poor W., whom you may remember my having mentioned in a former letter as having had a leg amputated a few weeks ago, and who was visiting us at the time, (he had been brought from the Empire in a rocking-chair,) looked like a marble statue of resignation. He possesses a face of uncommon beauty, and his large, dark eyes have always, I fancy, a sorrowful expression. Although he knew from the first shout what was about to happen, and was sitting on the couch which stood at that side of the cabin where the log must necessarily strike, and in his mutilated condition had, as he has since said, not the faintest hope of escape, yet the rich color for which he is remarkable paled not a shade during the whole affair.

The woodman who came so near causing a catastrophe was, I believe, infinitely more frightened than his might-have-been victims. He is a good-natured, stupid creature, and did not dare to descend the hill until some time after the excitement had subsided. The ludicrous expression of terror which his countenance wore when he came in to see what damage had been done, and to ask pardon for his carelessness, made us all laugh heartily.

W. related the almost miraculous escape of two persons from a similar danger last winter. The cabin, which was on Smith's Bar, was crushed into a mass of ruins almost in an instant, while an old man and his daughter, who were at dinner within its walls, remained sitting in the midst of the fallen logs, entirely unhurt.

The father immediately seized a gun and ran after the careless woodman, swearing that he would shoot him. Fortunately for the latter (for there is no doubt that in the first moments of his rage the old man would have slain him), his younger legs enabled him to make his escape, and he did not dare to return to the settlement for some days.

It has heretofore been a source of great interest to me to listen to the ringing sound of the ax, and the solemn crash of those majestic sentinels of the hills as they bow their green foreheads to the dust, but now I fear that I shall always hear them with a feeling of apprehension mingling with my former awe, although every one tells us that there is no danger of a repetition of the accident.

Last week there was a post-mortem examination of two men who died very suddenly in the neighborhood. Perhaps it will sound rather barbarous when I tell you that as there was no building upon the Bar which admitted light enough for the purpose, it was found necessary to conduct the examination in the open air, to the intense interest of the Kanakas, Indians, French, Spanish, English, Irish, and Yankees, who had gathered eagerly about the spot. Paganini Ned, with an anxious desire that Mrs. —— should be *amused* as much as possible in her mountain-home, rushed up from the kitchen, his dusky face radiant with excitement, to inform me that I could see both the bodies by just looking out of the window! I really frightened the poor fellow by the abrupt and vehement manner in which I declined taking advantage of his kindly hint.

One of the deceased was the husband of an American lady lecturess of the most intense description; and a strong-minded bloomer on the broadest principles.

Apropos, how *can* women, many of whom, I am told, are *really* interesting and intelligent,—how *can* they spoil their pretty mouths and ruin their beautiful complexions by demanding with Xanthippian *fervor*, in the presence, often, of a vulgar, irreverent mob, what the gentle creatures are pleased to call their "rights"? How *can* they wish to soil the delicate texture of their airy fancies by pondering over the wearying stupidities of Presidential elections, or the bewildering mystifications of rabid metaphysicians?

And, above all, *how* can they so far forget the sweet, shy coquetries of shrinking womanhood as to don those horrid bloomers? As for me, although a *wife*, I never wear the—well, you know what they call them when they wish to quiz henpecked husbands—even in the strictest privacy of life. I confess to an almost religious veneration for trailing drapery, and I pin my vestural faith with unflinching obstinacy to sweeping petticoats.

I knew a strong-minded bloomer at home, of some talent, and who was possessed, in a certain sense, of an excellent education. One day, after having flatteringly informed me that I really *had* a "soul above buttons" and the nursery, she gravely proposed that I should improve my *mind* by poring six hours a day over the metaphysical subtleties of Kant, Cousin, etc., and I remember that she called me a "piece of fashionable insipidity," and taunted me with not daring to go out of the beaten track, because I *truly* thought (for in those days I was an humble little thing enough, and sincerely desirous of walking in the right path as straitly as my feeble judgment would permit) that there were other authors more congenial to the flowerlike delicacy of the feminine intellect than her pet writers.

When will our sex appreciate the exquisite philosophy and truth of Lowell's remark upon the habits of Lady Redbreast and her esposo Robin, as illustrating the beautifully varied spheres of man and woman?—

He sings to the wide world, she to her nest;

In the nice ear of Nature, which song is the best?

Speaking of birds reminds me of a misfortune that I have lately experienced, which, in a life where there is so little to amuse and interest one, has been to me a subject of real grief. About three weeks ago, F. saw on the hill a California pheasant, which he chased into a coyote-hole and captured. Knowing how fond I am of pets, he brought it home and proposed that I should try to tame it.

Now, from earliest childhood I have resolutely refused to keep *wild* birds, and when I have had them given to me (which has happened several times in this country,—young bluebirds, etc.), I have invariably set them free, and I proposed doing the same with the pretty pheasant, but as they are the most delicately exquisite in flavor of all game, F. said that if I did not wish to keep it he would wring its neck and have it served up for dinner. With the cruelty of kindness— often more disastrous than that of real malice—I shrank from having it killed, and consented to let it run about the cabin.

It was a beautiful bird, a little larger than the domestic hen. Its slender neck, which it curved with haughty elegance, was tinted with various shades of a shining steel color. The large, bright eye glanced with the prettiest shyness at its captors, and the cluster of feathers forming its tail drooped with the rare grace of an ostrich-plume. The colors of the body were of a subdued brilliancy, reminding one of a rich but somber mosaic.

As it seemed very quiet, I really believed that in time we should be able to tame it. Still, it *would* remain constantly under the sofa or bedstead. So F. concluded to place it in a cage for a few hours of each day, in order that it might become gradually accustomed to our presence. This was done, the bird appearing as well as ever, and after closing the door of its temporary prison one day I left it and returned to my seat by the fire. In less than two minutes afterwards, a slight struggle in the cage attracted my attention. I ran hastily back, and you may imagine my distress when I found the beautiful pheasant lying lifeless upon the ground. It never breathed or showed the faintest sign of life afterwards.

You may laugh at me if you please, but I firmly believe that it died of homesickness. What wonder that the free, beautiful, happy creature of God, torn from the sight of the broad blue sky, the smiling river, and the fresh, fragrant fir-trees of its mountain-home, and shut up in a dark, gloomy cabin, should have broken in twain its haughty little heart? Yes, you may laugh, call me sentimental, etc., but I shall never forgive myself for having killed, by inches, in my selfish and cruel kindness, that pretty creature.

Many people here call this bird a grouse, and those who have crossed the plains say that it is very much like the prairie-hen. The Spanish name is gallina del campo, literally, hen of the field. Since the death of my poor little victim,

I have been told that it is utterly impossible to tame one of these birds, and it is said that if you put their eggs under a domestic fowl, the young, almost as soon as hatched, will instinctively run away to the beloved solitudes of their congenial homes, so passionately beats for liberty each pulse of their free and wild natures.

Among the noteworthy events which have occurred since my last, I don't know how I came to forget until the close of my letter two smart shocks of an earthquake to which we were treated a week ago. They were awe-inspiring, but, after all, were nothing in comparison to the timber-quake, an account of which I have given you above. But as F. is about to leave for the top of the Butte Mountains with a party of Rich Barians, and as I have much to do to prepare him for the journey, I must close.

Letter the Eleventh

[The Pioneer, December, 1854]

ROBBERY, TRIAL, EXECUTION—MORE TRAGEDY

SYNOPSIS

Theft of gold-dust. Arrest of two suspected miners. Trial and acquittal at miners' meeting. Robbed persons still believe accused guilty. Suspects leave mountains. One returns, and plan for his detection is successful. Confronted with evidence of guilt, discloses, on promise of immunity from prosecution, hiding-place of gold-dust. Miners, however, try him, and on conviction he is sentenced to be hanged one hour thereafter. Miners' mode of trial. Respite of three hours. Bungling execution. Drunken miner's proposal for sign of guilt or innocence. Corpse "enwrapped in white shroud of feathery snowflakes". Execution the work of the more reckless. Not generally approved. The Squire, disregarded, protested. Miners' procedure compared with the moderation of the first Vigilance Committee of San Francisco. Singular disappearance of body of miner. Returning to the States with his savings, his two companions report their leaving him in dying condition. Arrest and fruitless investigation. An unlikely bequest of money. Trial and acquittal of the miner's companions. Their story improbable, their actions like actual murder.

Letter the Eleventh

Robbery, Trial, Execution—More Tragedy

From our Log Cabin, Indian Bar,

December 15, 1851.

 I little thought, dear M., that here, with the "green watching hills" as witnesses, amid a solitude so grand and lofty that it seems as if the faintest whisper of passion must be hushed by its holy stillness, I should have to relate the perpetration of one of those fearful deeds which, were it for no other peculiarity than its startling suddenness, so utterly at variance with all *civilized* law, must make our beautiful California appear to strangers rather as a hideous phantom than the flower-wreathed reality which she is.

Whether the life which a few men, in the impertinent intoxication of power, have dared to crush out was worth that of a fly, I do not know,—perhaps not,—though God alone, methinks, can judge of the value of the soul upon which he has breathed. But certainly the effect upon the hearts of those who played the principal parts in the revolting scene referred to—a tragedy, in my simple judgment, so utterly useless—must be demoralizing in the extreme.

The facts in this sad case are as follows. Last fall, two men were arrested by their partners on suspicion of having stolen from them eighteen hundred dollars in gold-dust. The evidence was not sufficient to convict them, and they were acquitted. They were tried before a meeting of the miners, as at that time the law did not even *pretend* to wave its scepter over this place.

The prosecutors still believed them guilty, and fancied that the gold was hidden in a coyote-hole near the camp from which it had been taken. They therefore watched the place narrowly while the suspected men remained on the Bar. They made no discoveries, however, and soon after the trial the acquitted persons left the mountains for Marysville.

A few weeks ago, one of these men returned, and has spent most of the time since his arrival in loafing about the different barrooms upon the river. He is said to have been constantly intoxicated. As soon as the losers of the gold heard of his return, they bethought themselves of the coyote-hole, and placed about its entrance some brushwood and stones in such a manner that no one could go into it without disturbing the arrangement of them. In the mean while the thief settled at Rich Bar, and pretended that he was in search of some gravel-ground for mining purposes.

A few mornings ago he returned to his boarding-place, which he had left some hour earlier, with a spade in his hand, and, as he laid it down, carelessly observed that he had been out prospecting. The losers of the gold went, immediately after breakfast, as they had been in the habit of doing, to see if all was right at the coyote-hole. On this fatal day they saw that the entrance had been disturbed, and going in, they found upon the ground a money-belt which had apparently just been cut open. Armed with this evidence of guilt, they confronted the suspected person and sternly accused him of having the gold in his possession. Singularly enough, he did not attempt a denial, but said that if they would not bring him to a trial (which of course they promised) he would give it up immediately. He then informed them that they would find it beneath the blankets of his bunk, as those queer shelves on which miners sleep, ranged one above another somewhat like the berths of a ship, are generally called. There, sure enough, were six hundred dollars of the missing money, and the unfortunate wretch declared that his partner had taken the remainder to the States.

By this time the exciting news had spread all over the Bar. A meeting of the miners was immediately convened, the unhappy man taken into custody, a jury chosen, and a judge, lawyer, etc., appointed. Whether the men who had just regained a portion of their missing property made any objections to the proceedings which followed, I know not. If they had done so, however, it would have made no difference, as the *people* had taken the matter entirely out of their hands.

At one o'clock, so rapidly was the trial conducted, the judge charged the jury, and gently insinuated that they could do no less than to bring in with their verdict of guilty a sentence of *death*! Perhaps you know that when a trial is conducted without the majesty of the law, the jury are compelled to decide not only upon the guilt of the prisoner, but the mode of his punishment also. After a few minutes' absence, the twelve men, who had consented to burden their souls with a responsibility so fearful, returned, and the foreman handed to the judge a paper, from which he read the will of the *people*, as follows: That William Brown, convicted of stealing, etc., should, in *one hour* from that time, be hung by the neck until he was dead.

By the persuasions of some men more mildly disposed, they granted him a respite of *three hours* to prepare for his sudden entrance into eternity. He employed the time in writing, in his native language (he is a Swede), to some friends in Stockholm. God help them when that fatal post shall arrive, for, no doubt, *he* also, although a criminal, was fondly garnered in many a loving heart.

He had exhibited, during the trial, the utmost recklessness and nonchalance, had drank many times in the course of the day, and when the rope was placed about his neck, was evidently much intoxicated. All at once, however, he seemed startled into a consciousness of the awful reality of his position, and requested a few moments for prayer.

The execution was conducted by the jury, and was performed by throwing the cord, one end of which was attached to the neck of the prisoner, across the limb of a tree standing outside of the Rich Bar graveyard, when all who felt disposed to engage in so revolting a task lifted the poor wretch from the ground in the most awkward manner possible. The whole affair, indeed, was a piece of cruel butchery, though *that* was not intentional, but arose from the ignorance of those who made the preparations. In truth, life was only crushed out of him by hauling the writhing body up and down, several times in succession, by the rope, which was wound round a large bough of his green-leaved gallows. Almost everybody was surprised at the severity of the sentence, and many, with their hands on the cord, did not believe even *then* that it would be carried into effect, but thought that at the last moment the jury would release the prisoner and substitute a milder punishment.

It is said that the crowd generally seemed to feel the solemnity of the occasion, but many of the drunkards, who form a large part of the community on these bars, laughed and shouted as if it were a spectacle got up for their particular amusement. A disgusting specimen of intoxicated humanity, struck with one of those luminous ideas peculiar to his class, staggered up to the victim, who was praying at the moment, and, crowding a dirty rag into his almost unconscious hand, in a voice broken by a drunken hiccough, tearfully implored him to take his "hankercher," and if he were *innocent* (the man had not denied his guilt since first accused), to drop it as soon as he was drawn up into the air, but if *guilty*, not to let it fall on any account.

The body of the criminal was allowed to hang for some hours after the execution. It had commenced storming in the earlier part of the evening, and when those whose business it was to inter the remains arrived at the spot, they found them enwrapped in a soft white shroud of feathery snowflakes, as if pitying nature had tried to hide from the offended face of Heaven the cruel deed which her mountain-children had committed.

I have heard no one approve of this affair. It seems to have been carried on entirely by the more reckless part of the community. There is no doubt, however, that they seriously *thought* they were doing right, for many of them are kind and sensible men. They firmly believed that such an example was absolutely necessary for the protection of this community. Probably the recent case of Little John rendered this last sentence more severe than it otherwise would have been. The Squire, of course, could do nothing (as in criminal cases the *people* utterly refuse to acknowledge his authority) but protest against the whole of the proceedings, which he did in the usual legal manner.

If William Brown had committed a murder, or had even attacked a man for his money; if he had been a quarrelsome, fighting character, endangering lives in his excitement,—it would have been a very different affair. But, with the exception of the crime for which he perished (he *said* it was his first, and there is no reason to doubt the truth of his assertion), he was a harmless, quiet, inoffensive person.

You must not confound this miners' judgment with the doings of the noble Vigilance Committee of San Francisco. They are almost totally different in their organization and manner of proceeding. The Vigilance Committee had become absolutely necessary for the protection of society. It was composed of the best and wisest men in the city. They used their power with a moderation unexampled in history, and they laid it down with a calm and quiet readiness which was absolutely sublime, when they found that legal justice had again resumed that course of stern, unflinching duty which should always be its characteristic. They took ample time for a thorough investigation of all the circumstances relating to the criminals who fell into their hands, and in no case have they hung a man who had not been proved beyond the shadow of a doubt to have committed at least one robbery in which life had been endangered, if not absolutely taken.

But by this time, dear M., you must be tired of the melancholy subject, and yet if I keep my promise of relating to you all that interests *us* in our new and strange life, I shall have to finish my letter with a catastrophe in many respects more sad than that which I have just recounted.

At the commencement of our first storm, a hard-working, industrious laborer, who had accumulated about eight hundred dollars, concluded to return to the States. As the snow had been falling but a few hours when he, with two acquaintances, started from Rich Bar, no one doubted that they would not reach Marysville in perfect safety. They went on foot themselves, taking with them one mule to carry their blankets. For some unexplained reason, they took an unfrequented route. When the expressman came in, he said that he met the two companions of R. eight miles beyond Buck's Rancho, which is the first house one finds after leaving Rich Bar, and is only fourteen miles distant from here.

These men had camped at an uninhabited cabin called the "Frenchman's," where they had built a fire and were making themselves both merry and comfortable. They informed the expressman that they had left their *friend* (?) three miles back, in a dying state; that the cold had been too much for him, and that no doubt he was already dead. They had brought away the money, and even the *blankets*, of the expiring wretch! They said that if they had stopped with him they would have been frozen themselves. But even if their story is true, they must be the most brutal of creatures not to have made him as comfortable as possible, with *all* the blankets, and, after they had built their fire and got warm, to have returned and ascertained if he were really dead.

On hearing the expressman's report, several men who had been acquainted with the deceased started out to try and discover his remains. They found his violin, broken into several pieces, but all traces of the poor fellow himself had disappeared, probably forever.

In the mean while some travelers had carried the same news to Burke's Rancho, when several of the residents of that place followed the two men, and overtook them, to Bidwell's Bar, where they had them arrested on suspicion of murder. They protested their innocence, of course, and one of them said that he would lead a party to the spot where they had left the dying man. On arriving in the vicinity of the place, he at first stated that it was under one tree, then another, and another, and at last ended by declaring that it was utterly impossible for him to remember where they were camped at the time of R.'s death.

In this state of things, nothing was to be done but to return to B.'s, when, the excitement having somewhat subsided, they were allowed to proceed on their journey, the money, which they both swore R. had willed in his dying moments to a near relation of one of these very men, having been taken from them, in order to be sent by express to the friends of the deceased in the States.

Although they have been acquitted, many shake their heads doubtfully at the whole transaction. It seems very improbable that a man, accustomed all his life to hard labor and exposure, even although slightly unwell, as it is said he was, at the time, should have sunk under the cold during a walk of less than twenty miles, amid a gentle fall of snow and rain, when, as it is well known, the air is comparatively mild. It is to be hoped, however, that the companions of R. were brutal rather than criminal, though the desertion of a dying friend under such circumstances, even to the last unfeeling and selfish act of removing from the expiring creature his blankets, is, in truth, almost as bad as actual murder.

I hope, in my next, that I shall have something more cheerful than the above chapter of horrors to relate. In the mean while, adios, and think as kindly as you can of the dear California, even though her lustrous skies gaze upon such barbarous deeds.

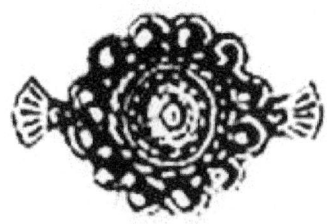

Letter the Twelfth

[The Pioneer, February, 1855]

A STORMY WINTER—HOLIDAY SATURNALIAS

SYNOPSIS

Saturnalia in camp. Temptations of riches. Tribute to the miners. Dreariness of camp-life during stormy winter weather. Christmas and change of proprietors at the Humboldt. Preparations for a double celebration. Mule-back loads of brandy-casks and champagne-baskets. Noisy procession of revelers. Oyster-and-champagne supper. Three days of revelry. Trial by mock vigilance committee. Judgment to "treat the crowd". Revels resumed on larger scale at New Year's. Boat-loads of drunken miners fall into river. Saved by being drunk. Boat-load of bread falls into river and floats down-stream. Pulley-and-rope device for hauling boat across river. Fiddlers "nearly fiddled themselves into the grave". Liquors "beginning to look scarce". Subdued and sheepish-looking bacchanals. Nothing extenuated, nor aught set down in malice. Boating on the river. Aquatic plants. Bridge swept away in torrent. Loss of canoe. Branch from moss-grown fir-tree "a cornice wreathed with purple-starred tapestry". A New Year's present from the river. A two-inch spotted trout. No fresh meat for a month. "Dark and ominous rumors". Dark hams, rusty pork, etc., stored.

Letter the Twelfth
A Stormy Winter—Holiday Saturnalias
From our Log Cabin, Indian Bar,
January 27, 1852.

I wish that it were possible, dear M., to give you an idea of the perfect saturnalia which has been held upon the river for the last three weeks, without at the same time causing you to think *too* severely of our good mountains. In truth, it requires not only a large intellect, but a large heart, to judge with becoming charity of the peculiar temptations of riches. A more generous, hospitable, intelligent, and industrious people than the inhabitants of the half-dozen bars, of which Rich Bar is the nucleus, never existed; for you know how proverbially wearing it is to the nerves of manhood to be entirely without either occupation or amusement, and that has been preeminently the case during the present month.

Imagine a company of enterprising and excitable young men, settled upon a sandy level about as large as a poor widow's potato-patch, walled in by sky-kissing hills, absolutely *compelled* to remain on account of the weather, which has vetoed indefinitely their exodus, with no place to ride or drive even if they had the necessary vehicles and quadrupeds; with no newspapers nor politics to interest them; deprived of all books but a few dog-eared novels of the poorest class,—churches, lectures, lyceums, theaters, and (most unkindest cut of all!) pretty girls, having become to these unhappy men mere myths; without *one* of the thousand ways of passing time peculiar to civilization, most of them living in damp, gloomy cabins, where heaven's dear light can enter only by the door; and when you add to all these disagreeables the fact that, during the never-to-be-forgotten month, the most remorseless, persevering rain which ever set itself to work to drive humanity mad has been pouring doggedly down, sweeping away bridges, lying in uncomfortable puddles about nearly all of the habitations, wickedly insinuating itself beneath un-umbrella-protected shirt-collars, generously treating to a shower-bath *and* the rheumatism sleeping bipeds who did not happen to have an india-rubber blanket, and, to crown all, rendering mining utterly impossible,—you cannot wonder that even the most moral should have become somewhat reckless.

The saturnalia commenced on Christmas evening, at the Humboldt, which, on that very day, had passed into the hands of new proprietors. The most gorgeous preparations were made for celebrating the *two* events. The bar was retrimmed with red calico, the bowling-alley had a new lining of the coarsest and whitest cotton cloth, and the broken lamp-shades were replaced by whole ones. All day long, patient mules could be seen descending the hill, bending beneath casks of brandy and baskets of champagne, and, for the first time in the history of that celebrated building, the floor (wonderful to relate, it *has* a floor) was *washed*, at a lavish expenditure of some fifty pails of water, the using up of one entire broom, and the melting away of sundry bars of the best yellow soap, after which I am told that the enterprising and benevolent individuals who had undertaken the herculean task succeeded in washing the boards through the hopeless load of dirt which had accumulated upon them during the summer and autumn. All these interesting particulars were communicated to me by Ned when he brought up dinner. That distinguished individual himself was in his element, and in a most intense state of perspiration and excitement at the same time.

About dark we were startled by the loudest hurrahs, which arose at the sight of an army of india-rubber coats (the rain was falling in riverfuls), each one enshrouding a Rich Barian, which was rapidly descending the hill. This troop was headed by the "General," who, lucky man that he is, waved on high, instead of a banner, a *live* lantern, actually composed of tin and window-glass, and evidently intended by its maker to act in no capacity but that *of* a lantern. The General is the largest and tallest, and with one exception I think the oldest, man upon the river. He is about fifty, I should fancy, and wears a snow-white beard of such immense dimensions, in both length and thickness, that any elderly Turk would expire with envy at the mere sight of it. Don't imagine that *he* is a reveler. By no means. The gay crowd followed *him*, for the same reason that the king followed Madam Blaize,—because she went before.

At nine o'clock in the evening they had an oyster-and-champagne supper in the Humboldt, which was very gay with toasts, songs, speeches, etc. I believe that the company danced all night. At any rate, they were dancing when I went to sleep, and they were dancing when I woke the next morning. The revel was kept up in this mad way for three days, growing wilder every hour. Some never slept at all during that time. On the fourth day they got past dancing, and, lying in drunken heaps about the barroom, commenced a most unearthly howling. Some barked like dogs, some roared like bulls, and others hissed like serpents and geese. Many were too far gone to imitate anything but their own animalized selves. The scene, from the description I have had of it, must have been a complete illustration of the fable of Circe and her fearful transformations. Some of these bacchanals were among the most respectable and respected men upon the river. Many of them had resided here for more than a year, and had never been seen intoxicated before. It seemed as if they were seized with a reckless mania for pouring down liquor, which, as I said above, everything conspired to foster and increase.

Of course there were some who kept themselves aloof from these excesses, but they were few, and were not allowed to enjoy their sobriety in peace. The revelers formed themselves into a mock vigilance committee, and when one of these unfortunates appeared outside, a constable, followed by those who were able to keep their legs, brought him before the court, where he was tried on some amusing charge, and *invariably* sentenced to "treat the crowd." The prisoners had generally the good sense to submit cheerfully to their fate.

Towards the latter part of the week, people were compelled to be a little more quiet, from sheer exhaustion, but on New Year's Day, when there was a grand dinner at Rich Bar, the excitement broke out, if possible, worse than ever. The same scenes, in a more or less aggravated form, in proportion as the strength of the actors held out, were repeated at Smith's Bar and The Junction.

Nearly every day I was dreadfully frightened by seeing a boat-load of intoxicated men fall into the river, where nothing but the fact of their *being* intoxicated saved many of them from drowning. One morning about thirty dollars' worth of bread (it must have been tipsy-cake), which the baker was conveying to Smith's Bar, fell overboard, and sailed merrily away towards Marysville. People passed the river in a boat, which was managed by a pulley and a rope that was strained across it from Indian Bar to the opposite shore.

Of the many acquaintances who had been in the habit of calling nearly evening, three, only, appeared in the cabin during as many weeks. Now, however, the saturnalia is about over. Ned and Chock have nearly fiddled themselves into their respective graves, the claret (a favorite wine with miners) and oysters are exhausted, brandied fruits are rarely seen, and even port-wine is beginning to look scarce. Old callers occasionally drop in, looking dreadfully sheepish and subdued, and so *sorry*, and people are evidently arousing themselves from the bacchanal madness into which they were so suddenly and so strangely drawn.

With the exception of my last, this is the most unpleasant letter which I have ever felt it my duty to write to you. Perhaps you will wonder that I should touch upon such a disagreeable subject at all. But I am bound, Molly, by my promise to give you a *true* picture (as much as in me lies) of mining-life and its peculiar temptations, nothing extenuating, nor setting down aught in malice. But, with all their failings, believe me, the miners, as a class, possess many truly admirable characteristics.

I have had rather a stupid time during the storm. We have been in the habit of taking frequent rows upon the river, in a funny little toppling canoe carved out of a log. The bridge at one end of our boating-ground, and the rapids at the other, made quite a pretty lake. To be sure, it was so small that we generally passed and repassed its beautiful surface at least thirty times in an hour. But we did not mind *that*, I can assure you. We were only *too* glad to be able to go onto the water at all. I used to return loaded down with the magnificent large leaves of some aquatic plant which the gentle frosts had painted with the most gorgeous colors, lots of fragrant mint, and a few wan white flowers which had lingered past their autumnal glory. The richest hothouse bouquet could never give me half the pleasure which I took in arranging, in a pretty vase of purple and white, those gorgeous leaves. They made me think of Moorish arabesques, so quaint and bizarre, and at the same time dazzlingly brilliant, were the varied tints. They were in their glory at evening, for, like an oriental beauty, they lighted up splendidly. Alas! where, one little month ago, my little lake lay laughing up at the stars, a turbid torrent rushes noisily by. The poor little canoe was swept away with the bridge, and splendid leaves hide their bright heads forever beneath the dark waters.

But I am not entirely bereft of the beautiful. From my last walk I brought home a tiny bit of outdoors, which, through all the long, rainy months that are to come, will sing to me silently, yet eloquently, of the blue and gold of the vanished summer, and the crimson and purple of its autumn. It is a branch, gathered from that prettiest feature of mountain scenery,—a moss-grown fir-tree. You will see them at every step, standing all-lovely in this graceful robe. It is, in color, a vivid pea-green, with little hard flowers which look more like dots than anything else, and contrast beautifully with the deeper verdure of the fir. The branch which I brought home I have placed above my window. It is three feet in length, and as large round as a person's arm; and there it remains, a cornice wreathed with purple-starred tapestry, whose wondrous beauty no upholsterer can ever match.

I have got the prettiest New Year's present. You will never guess what it is, so I shall have to tell you. On the eve of the year, as the "General" was lifting a glass of water, which had just been brought from the river, to his lips, he was startled at the sight of a tiny fish. He immediately put it into a glass jar and gave it to me. It is that most lovely of all the creatures of Thetis, a spotted trout, a little more than two inches in length. Its back, of mingled green and gold, is splashed with dots of the richest sable. A mark of a dark-ruby color, in shape like an anchor, crowns its elegant little head. Nothing can be prettier than the delicate wings of pale purple with which its snowy belly is faintly penciled. Its jet-black eyes, rimmed with silver within a circlet of rare sea-blue, gleam like diamonds, and its whole graceful shape is gilded with a shimmering sheen infinitely lovely. When I watch it from across the room as it glides slowly round its crystal palace, it reminds me of a beam of many-colored light, but when it glides up and down in its gay playfulness, it gleams through the liquid atmosphere like a box of shining silver. "A thing of beauty is a joy forever," and truly I never weary watching the perfected loveliness of my graceful little captive.

In the list of my deprivations above written, I forgot to mention a fact which I know will gain me the sympathy of all carnivorously disposed people. It is, that we have had no fresh meat for nearly a month! Dark and ominous rumors are also floating through the moist air, to the effect that the potatoes and onions are about to give out! But don't be alarmed, dear Molly. There is no danger of a famine. For have we not got wagon-loads of hard, dark hams, whose indurated hearts nothing but the sharpest knife and the stoutest arm can penetrate? Have we not got quintals of dreadful mackerel, fearfully crystallized in black salt? Have we not barrels upon barrels of rusty pork, and flour enough to victual a large army for the next two years? Yea, verily, have we, and more also. For we have oysters in cans, preserved meats, and sardines (apropos, I *detest* them), by the hundred-boxful.

So, hush the trembling of that tender little heart, and shut those tearful and alarmed eyes while I press a good-night kiss On their drooping lids.

Letter the Thirteenth
[The Pioneer, March, 1855]
SOCIABILITY and EXCITEMENTS of MINING-LIFE
SYNOPSIS

Departure Indian Bar of the mulatto Ned. His birthday-celebration dinner, at which the New Year's piscatory phenomenon figures in the bill of fare. A total disregard of dry laws at the dinner. Excitement over reported discovery of quartz-mines. A complete humbug. Charges of salting. Excitement renewed upon report of other new quartz-mines. Even if rich, lack of proper machinery would render working thereof impossible. Prediction that quartz-mines eventually will be the most profitable. Miners decamp without paying their debts. Pursuit and capture. Miners' court orders settlement in full. Celebration, by French miners, of the Revolution of 1848. Invitation to dine at best-built log cabin on the river. The habitation of five or six young miners. A perfect marvel of a fireplace. Huge unsplit logs as firewood. Window of glass jars. Possibilities in the use of empty glass containers. Unthrift of some miners. The cabin, its furniture, store of staple provisions, chinaware, cutlery. The dinner in the cabin. A cow kept. Wonderful variety of makeshift candlesticks in use among the miners. Dearth of butter, potatoes, onions, fresh meat, in camp. Indian-summer weather at Indian Bar. A cozy retreat in the hills. A present of feathered denizens of the mountains. Roasted for dinner.

Letter the Thirteenth
Sociability and Excitements of Mining-life
From our Log Cabin, Indian Bar,
February 27, 1852.

 You will find this missive, dear M., a journal, rather than a letter; for the few insignificant events which have taken place since I last wrote to you will require but three lines apiece for their recital. But stop; when I say "insignificant" I forget one all-important misfortune which, for our sins I suppose, has befallen us, in the sudden departure of our sable Paganini.

Yes; Vattal Ned to the valley hath gone,
In a Marysville kitchen you'll find him;
Two rusty pistols he girded on,
And his violin hung behind him.

His fiddle is heard no more on all the Bar, and silence reigns through the calico halls of the Humboldt. His bland smile and his dainty plats, his inimitably choice language and his pet tambourine, his woolly corkscrew and his really beautiful music, have, I fear, vanished forever from the mountains.

Just before he left he found a birthday which belonged to himself, and was observed all the morning thereof standing about in spots, a perfect picture of perplexity painted in burnt umber. Inquiry being made by sympathizing friends as to the cause of his distress, he answered, that, having no fresh meat, he could not prepare a dinner for the log cabin, worthy of the occasion!

But no circumstance can put a man of genius entirely *hors de combat*. Confine him in a dungeon, banish him to an uninhabited island, place him, solitary and alone, in a boundless desert, deprive him of all but life, and he will still achieve wonders. With the iron hams, the piscatory phenomenon referred to in my last, and a can of really excellent oysters, Ned's birthday dinner was a *chef-d'oeuvre*. He accompanied it with a present of a bottle of very good champagne, requesting us to drink it (which we *did*, not having the fear of temperance societies or Maine-law liquor bills before our eyes) in honor of his having dropped another year into the returnless past.

There has been a great excitement here on account of the fancied discovery of valuable quartz-mines in the vicinity of the American Rancho, which is situated about twenty miles from this place. Half the people upon the river went out there for the purpose of prospecting and staking claims. The quartz apparently paid admirably. Several companies were speedily formed, and men sent to Hamilton, the county seat, to record the various claims. F. himself went out there, and remained several days. Now, however, the whole excitement has turned out to be a complete humbug. The quicksilver which was procured at the rancho for the testing of the quartz, the victims declare, was salted, and they accuse the rancheros of conniving at the fraud for the purpose of making money out of those who were compelled to lodge and board with them while prospecting. The accused affirm that if there was any deception (which, however, is beyond the shadow of a doubt), they also were deceived; and as they appear like honest men enough, I am inclined to believe them.

Just now there is a new quartz-mine excitement. A man has engaged to lead a company to the golden and crystallized spot. Probably this also will prove, like the other, a mere yellow bubble. But, even if as rich as he says, it will be of little value at present, on account of the want of suitable machinery, that now in use being so expensive and wasting so much of the precious metal that it leaves the miner but little profit. It is thought, however, by men of judgment that in a few years, when the proper way of working them to advantage has been discovered, the quartz-mines will be more profitable than any others in California.

A few days ago we had another specimen of illegal, but in this case at least extremely equitable, justice. Five men left the river without paying their debts. A meeting of the miners was convened, and "Yank," who possesses an iron frame, the perseverance of a bulldog, and a constitution which never knew fatigue, was appointed, with another person, to go in search of the culprits and bring them back to Indian Bar. He found them a few miles from this place, and returned with them in triumph, and alone, his friend having been compelled to remain behind on account of excessive fatigue. The self-constituted court, after a fair trial, obliged the five men to settle all liabilities before they again left the river.

Last week the Frenchmen on the river celebrated the Revolution of February, 1848. What kind of a time they had during the day, I know not, but in the evening (apropos, part of them reside at Missouri Bar) they formed a torchlight procession and marched to Rich Bar, which, by the way, takes airs upon itself, and considers itself a *town*. They made quite a picturesque appearance as they wound up the hill, each one carrying a tiny pine-tree, the top of which was encircled with a diadem of flame, beautifully lighting up the darker verdure beneath, and gleaming like a spectral crown through the moonless, misty evening. We could not help laughing at their watchwords. They ran in this wise: Shorge Washingtone, James K. Polk, Napoleon Bonaparte! Liberté, égalité, fraternité! Andrew Jacksone, President Fillmore, and Lafayette! I give them to you word for word, as I took them down at the time.

Since the bridges have been swept away, I have been to Rich Bar but once. It is necessary to go over the hill now, and the walk is a very wearisome one. It is much more pleasant to live on the hills than on the Bar, and during our walk we passed two or three cozy little cabins, nestling in broad patches of sunlight, and surrounded with ample space for a promenade, which made me quite envious. Unfortunately, F.'s profession renders it desirable that he should reside where the largest number of people congregate, and then the ascent to the habitable portion of the hill is as steep as any part of that leading into

Rich Bar, and it would be impossible for him to walk up and down it several times a day,—a task which he would be compelled to perform if we resided there. For that reason I make myself as happy as possible where I am.

I have been invited to dine at the best-built log cabin on the river. It is situated on the hill of which I have just been writing, and is owned by five or six intelligent, hard-working, sturdy young men. Of course it has no floor, but it boasts a perfect marvel of a fireplace. They never pretend to split the wood for it, but merely fall a giant fir-tree, strip it of its branches, and cut it into pieces the length of the aforesaid wonder. This cabin is lighted in a manner truly ingenious. Three feet in length of a log on one side of the room is removed and glass jars inserted in its place, the space around the necks of said jars being filled in with clay. This novel idea is really an excellent substitute for window-glass. You will perhaps wonder where they procure enough of the material for such a purpose. They are brought here in enormous quantities, containing brandied fruits, for there is no possible luxury connected with drinking, which is procurable in California, that cannot be found in the mines, and the very men who fancy it a piece of wicked extravagance to *buy* bread, because they can save a few dimes by *making* it themselves, are often those who think nothing of spending from fifteen to twenty dollars a night in the bar-rooms. There is at this moment a perfect Pelion-upon-Ossa-like pile of beautiful glass jars, porter, ale, champagne, and claret bottles, lying in front of my window. The latter are a very convenient article for the manufacture of the most enchantingly primitive lanterns. Any one in want of a utensil of this kind has but to step to his cabin-door, take up a claret or champagne bottle, knock off the bottom, and dropping into the neck thereof, through the opening thus made, a candle, to have a most excellent lantern. And the beauty of it is, that, every time you wish to use such a thing, you can have a *new* one.

But to return to my description of the cabin. It consists of one very large room, in the back part of which are neatly stored several hundred sacks of flour, a large quantity of potatoes, sundry kegs of butter, and plenty of hams and mackerel. The furniture consists of substantial wooden stools, and in these I observed that our friends followed the fashion, no two of them being made alike. Some stood proudly forth in all the grandeur of four legs, others affected the classic grace of the ancient tripod, while a few shrank bashfully into corners on one stubbed stump. Some round, some square, and some triangular in form. Several were so high that, when enthroned upon them, the ends of my toes just touched the ground, and others were so low that, on rising, I carried away a large portion of the soil upon my unfortunate skirts. Their bunks, as they call them, were arranged in two rows along one side of the cabin, each neatly covered with a dark-blue or red blanket. A handsome oilcloth was spread upon the table, and the service consisted of tin plates, a pretty set of stone-china cups and saucers, and some good knives and forks, which looked almost as bright as if they had just come from the cutler's. For dinner we had boiled beef and ham, broiled mackerel, potatoes, splendid new bread made by one of the gentlemen of the house, coffee, milk (Mr. B. has bought a cow, and now and then we get a wee drop of milk), and the most delicious Indian meal, parched, that I ever tasted. I have been very particular in describing this cabin, for it is the best-built and by far the best-appointed one upon the river.

I have said nothing about candlesticks as yet. I must confess that in *them* the spice of life is carried almost too far. One gets satiated with their wonderful variety. I will mention but two or three of these makeshifts. Bottles, *without* the bottoms knocked off, are general favorites. Many, however, exhibit an insane admiration for match-boxes, which, considering that they *will* keep falling *all* the time, and leaving the entire house in darkness, and scattering spermaceti in every direction, is rather an inconvenient taste. Some fancy blocks of wood with an ornamental balustrade of three nails, and I *have* seen praiseworthy candles making desperate efforts to stand straight in tumblers! Many of our friends, with a beautiful and sublime faith in spermaceti and good luck, eschew everything of the kind, and you will often find their tables picturesquely covered with splashes of the former article, elegantly ornamented with little strips of black wick.

The sad forebodings mentioned in a former letter have come to pass. For some weeks, with the exception of two or three families, every one upon the river has been out of butter, onions, and potatoes. Our kind friends upon the hill, who have a little remaining, sent me a few pounds of the former the other day. Ham, mackerel, and bread, with occasionally a treat of the precious butter, have been literally our only food for a long time. The rancheros have not driven in any beef for several weeks, and although it is so pleasant on the bars, the cold on the mountains still continues so intense that the trail remained impassable to mules.

The weather here for the past five weeks has been like the Indian summer at home. Nearly every day I take a walk up onto the hill back of our cabin. Nobody lives there, it is so very steep. I have a cozy little seat in the fragrant bosom of some evergreen shrubs, where often I remain for hours. It is almost like death to mount to my favorite spot, the path is so steep and stony; but it is new life, when I arrive there, to sit in the shadow of the pines and listen to the plaintive wail of the wind as it surges through their musical leaves, and to gaze down upon the tented Bar lying in somber gloom (for as yet the sun does not shine upon it) and the foam-flaked river, and around at the awful mountain splashed here and there with broad patches of snow, or reverently upward into the stainless blue of our unmatchable sky.

This letter is much longer than I thought it would be when I commenced it, and I believe that I have been as minutely particular as even you can desire. I have mentioned everything that has happened since I last wrote. Oh! I was very near forgetting a present of two ring-doves (alas! they had been shot) and a blue jay which I received yesterday. We had them roasted for dinner last evening. The former were very beautiful, approaching in hue more nearly to a French gray than what is generally called a dun color, with a perfect ring of ivory encircling each pretty neck. The blue jay was exactly like its namesake in the States.

Good by, my dear M., and remember that the *same* sky, though not quite so beautiful a portion of it, which smiles upon *me* in sunny California bends lovingly over *you* in cold, dreary, but, in spite of its harsh airs, beloved New England.

Letter the Fourteenth

[The Pioneer, April, 1855]

SPRINGTIDE—LINGUISTICS—STORMS—ACCIDENTS

SYNOPSIS

The splendor of a March morning in the mountains of California. First bird of the season. Blue and red shirted miners a feature of the landscape. "Wanderers from the whole broad earth". The languages of many nations heard. How the Americans attempt to converse with the Spanish-speaking population. "Sabe," "vamos," "poco tiempo," "si," and "bueno," a complete lexicon of la lengua castellana, in mind of Americans. An "ugly disposition" manifested when the speaker is not understood. Spaniards "ain't kinder like our folks," nor "folksy". Mistakes not all on one side. Spanish proverb regarding certain languages. Not complimentary to English. Stormy weather. Storm king a perfect Proteus. River on a rampage. Sawmill carried away. Pastimes of the miners during the storm. MS. account of storm sent in keg via river to Marysville newspaper. Silversmith makes gold rings during storm. Raffling and reraffling of same as pastime. Some natural gold rings. Nugget in shape of eagle's head presented to author. Miners buried up to neck in cave-in. Escape with but slight injury. Miner stabbed without provocation in drunken frolic. Life despaired of at first. No notice taken of affair.

Letter the Fourteenth

Springtide—Linguistics—Storms—Accidents

From our Log Cabin, Indian Bar,

March 15, 1852.

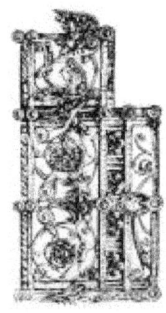

This fifteenth day of March has risen upon us with all the primeval splendor of the birth-morn of creation. The lovely river, having resumed its crimson border (the so long idle miners being again busily at work), glides by, laughing gayly, leaping and clapping its glad waves joyfully in the golden sunlight. The feathery fringe of the fir-trees glitters like emerald in the luster-bathing air. A hundred tiny rivulets flash down from the brow of the mountains, as if some mighty Titan, standing on the other side, had flung athwart their greenness a chaplet of radiant pearls. Of the large quantities of snow which have fallen within the past fortnight, a few patches of shining whiteness, high up among the hills, alone remain, while, to finish the picture, the lustrous heaven of California, looking farther off than ever through the wonderfully transparent atmosphere, and for that very reason infinitely more beautiful, bends over all the matchless blue of its resplendent arch. Ah, the heaven of the Golden Land! To you, living beneath the murky skies of New England, how unimaginably lovely it is. A small poetess has said that *she* could not love a scene where the blue sky was *always* blue. I think it is not so with me. I am sure I never weary of the succession of rainless months, nor of the azure dome, day after day so mistless, which bends above this favored country.

Between each stroke of the pen I stop to glance at that splendor, whose sameness never fails, but now a flock of ring-doves break for a moment with dots of purple its monotonous beauty, and the carol of a tiny bird (the first of the season), though I cannot see the darling, fills the joyful air with its matin song.

All along the side of the hill behind the Bar, and on the latter also, glance spots of azure and crimson, in the forms of blue and red shirted miners bending steadily over pickax and shovel, reminding one involuntarily of the muck-gatherer in The Pilgrim's Progress. But no; that is an unjust association of ideas, for many of these men are toiling thus wearily for laughing-lipped children, calm-browed wives, or saintly mothers, gathering around the household hearth in some far-away country. Even among the few now remaining on the river there are wanderers from the whole broad earth, and, oh, what a world of poetic recollection is suggested by their living presence! From happiest homes and such luxuriant lands has the golden magnet drawn its victims. From those palm-girdled isles of the Pacific, which Melville's gifted pen has consecrated to such beautiful romance; from Indies, blazing through the dim past with funeral pyres, upon whose perfumed flame ascended to God the chaste souls of her devoted wives; from the grand old woods of classic Greece, haunted by nymph and satyr, Naiad and Grace, grape-crowned Bacchus and beauty-zoned Venus; from the polished heart of artificial Europe; from the breezy backwoods of young America; from the tropical languor of Asian savannah; *from* every spot shining through the rosy light of beloved old fables, or consecrated by lofty deeds of heroism or devotion, or shrined in our heart of hearts as the sacred home of some great or gifted one,—they gather to the golden harvest.

You will hear in the same day, almost at the same time, the lofty melody of the Spanish language, the piquant polish of the French (which, though not a *musical* tongue, is the most *useful* of them all), the silver, changing clearness of the Italian, the harsh gangle of the German, the hissing precision of the English, the liquid sweetness of the Kanaka, and the sleep-inspiring languor of the East Indian. To complete the catalogue, there is the *native* Indian, with his guttural vocabulary of twenty words! When I hear these sounds, so strangely different, and look at the speakers, I fancy them a living polyglot of the languages, a perambulating picture-gallery illustrative of national variety in form and feature.

By the way, speaking of languages, nothing is more amusing than to observe the different styles in which the generality of Americans talk *at* the unfortunate Spaniard. In the first place, many of them really believe that when they have learned *sabe* and *vamos* (two words which they seldom use in the right place), *poco tiempo*, *si*, and *bueno* (the last they *will* persist in pronouncing whayno), they have the whole of the glorious Castilian at their tongue's end. Some, however, eschew the above words entirely, and innocently fancy that by splitting the tympanum of an unhappy foreigner in screaming forth their sentences in good solid English they can be surely understood; others, at the imminent risk of dislocating their own limbs, and the jaws of their listeners by the laughs which their efforts elicit, make the most excruciatingly grotesque gestures, and think *that* that is speaking Spanish. The majority, however, place a most beautiful and touching faith in *broken English*, and when they murder it with the few words of Castilian quoted above, are firmly convinced that it is nothing but their "ugly dispositions" which make the Spaniards pretend not to understand them.

One of those dear, stupid Yankees who *will* now and then venture out of sight of the smoke of their own chimneys as far as California, was relating *his* experience in this particular the other day. It seems he had lost a horse somewhere among the hills, and during his search for it met a gentlemanly Chileño, who with national suavity made the most desperate efforts to understand the questions put to him. Of course Chileño was so stupid that he did not succeed, for it is not possible one of the Great American People could fail to express himself clearly even in Hebrew if he takes it into his cute head to speak that ancient but highly respectable language. Our Yankee friend, however, would not allow the poor fellow even the excuse of stupidity, but declared that he only "played possum from sheer *ugliness*." "Why," he added, in relating the circumstance, "the cross old rascal pretended not to understand his own language, though I said as plainly as possible,

'Señor, sabe mi horso vamos poco tiempo?' which, perhaps you don't know," he proceeded to say, in a benevolent desire to enlighten our ignorance and teach us a little Castilian, "means, 'Sir, I have lost my horse; have you seen it?'" I am ashamed to acknowledge that we did *not* know the above-written Anglo-Spanish meant *that*! The honest fellow concluded his story by declaring (and it is a common remark with uneducated Americans) with a most self-glorifying air of *pity* for the poor Spaniards, "They ain't kinder like *eour* folks," or, as that universal Aunt Somebody used so expressively to observe, "Somehow, they ain't *folksy*!"

The mistakes made on the other side are often quite as amusing. Dr. Cañas related to us a laughable anecdote of a countryman of his, with whom he happened to camp on his first arrival in San Francisco. None of the party could speak a word of English, and the person referred to, as ignorant as the rest, went out to purchase bread, which he procured by laying down some money and pointing to a loaf of that necessary edible. He probably heard a person use the words "some bread," for he rushed home, Cañas said, in a perfect burst of newly acquired wisdom, and informed his friends that he had found out the English for "pan," and that when they wished any of that article they need but enter a bakeshop and utter the word "sombrero" in order to obtain it! His hearers were delighted to know *that* much of the *infernal lengua*, greatly marveling, however, that the same word which meant "hat" in Castilian should mean "bread" in English. The Spaniards have a saying to the following effect: "Children speak in Italian, ladies speak in French, God speaks in Spanish, and the Devil speaks in English."

I commenced this letter with the intention of telling you about the weary, weary storm, which has not only thrown a damp over our spirits, but has saturated them, as it has everything else, with a deluge of moisture. The storm king commenced his reign (or rain) on the 28th of February, and proved himself a perfect Proteus during his residence with us. For one entire week he descended daily and nightly, without an hour's cessation, in a forty Niagara-power of water, and just as we were getting reconciled to this wet state of affairs, and were thinking seriously of learning to swim, one gloomy evening, when we least expected such a change, he stole softly down and garlanded us in a wreath of shiny snowflakes, and lo! the next morning you would have thought that some great white bird had shed its glittering feathers all over rock, tree, hill, and bar. He finished his vagaries by loosening, rattling, and crashing upon this devoted spot a small skyful of hailstones, which, aided by a terrific wind, waged terrible warfare against the frail tents and the calico-shirt huts, and made even the shingles on the roofs of the log cabins tremble amid their nails.

The river, usually so bland and smiling, looked really terrific. It rose to an unexampled height, and tore along its way, a perfect mass of dark-foamed turbid waves. At one time we had serious fears that the water would cover the whole Bar, for it approached within two or three feet of the Humboldt. A sawmill, which had been built at a great expense by two gentlemen of Rich Bar in order to be ready for the sawing of lumber for the extensive fluming operations which are in contemplation this season, was entirely swept away, nearly ruining, it is said, the owners. I heard a great shout early one morning, and, running to the window, had the sorrow to see wheels, planks, etc., sailing merrily down the river. All along the banks of the stream, men were trying to save the more valuable portions of the mill, but the torrent was so furious that it was utterly impossible to rescue a plank. How the haughty river seemed to laugh to scorn the feeble efforts of man! How its mad waves tossed in wild derision the costly workmanship of his skillful hands! But know, proud Río de las Plumas, that these very men whose futile efforts you fancy that you have for once so gloriously defeated will gather from beneath your lowest depths the beautiful ore which you thought you had hidden forever and forever beneath your azure beauty!

It is certainly most amusing to hear of the different plans which the poor miners invented to pass the time during the trying season of rains. Of course, poker and euchre, whist and ninepins, to say nothing of monte and faro, are now in constant requisition. But as a person would starve to death on *toujours des perdrix*, so a man cannot *always* be playing cards. Some *literary* bipeds, I have been told, reduced to the last degree of intellectual destitution, in a beautiful spirit of self-martyrdom betook themselves to blue blankets, bunks, and Ned Buntline's novels. And one day an unhappy youth went pen-mad, and in a melancholy fit of authorship wrote a thrilling account of our dreadful situation, which, directed to the editor of a Marysville paper, was sealed up in a keg and set adrift, and is at this moment, no doubt, stranded, high and dry, in the streets of Sacramento, for it is generally believed that the cities of the plain have been under water during the storm. The chief amusement, however, has been the raffling of gold rings. There is a silversmith here, who, like the rest of the miserable inhabitants, having nothing to do, discovered that he could make gold rings. Of course every person must have a specimen of his workmanship, and the next thing was to raffle it off, the winner generally repeating the operation. Nothing was done or talked of for some days but this important business.

I have one of these rings, which is really very beautifully finished, and although perhaps at home it would look vulgar, there is a sort of massive and barbaric grandeur about it which seems well suited to our wild life of the hills. I shall send you one of these, which will be to you a curiosity, and will doubtless look strangely enough amid the graceful and airy politeness of French jewelry. But I think that it will be interesting to you, as having been manufactured in the mines by an inexperienced workman, and without the necessary tools. If it is too hideous to be worn upon your slender little finger, you can have it engraved for a seal, and attach it as a charm to your watch-chain.

Last evening Mr. C. showed us a specimen ring which he had just finished. It is the handsomest *natural* specimen that I ever saw. Pure gold is generally dull in hue, but this is of a most beautiful shade of yellow, and extremely brilliant. It is, in shape and size, exactly like the flower of the jonquil. In the center is inserted, with all the nice finish of art (or rather of nature, for it is her work), a polished piece of quartz, of the purest shade of pink, and between each radiant petal is set a tiny crystal of colorless quartz, every one of which flashes like a real diamond. It is known beyond doubt to be a real live specimen, as many saw it when it was first taken from the earth, and the owner has carried it carelessly in his pocket for months. We would gladly have given fifty dollars for it, though its nominal value is only about an ounce, but it is already promised as a present to a gentleman in Marysville. Although rather a clumsy ring, it would make a most unique brooch, and indeed is almost the *only* piece of unmanufactured ore which I have ever seen that I would be willing to wear. I have a piece of gold which, without any alteration, except, of course, engraving, will make a beautiful seal. It is in the shape of an eagle's head, and is wonderfully perfect. It was picked up from the surface of the ground by a gentleman on his first arrival here, and he said that he would give it to the next lady to whom he should be introduced. He carried it in his purse for more than a year, when, in obedience to the promise made when he found it, it became the property of your humble servant, Shirley.

The other day a hole caved in, burying up to the neck two unfortunates who were in it at the time. Luckily, they were but slightly injured. F. is at present attending a man at The Junction, who was stabbed very severely in the back during a drunken frolic. The people have not taken the slightest notice of this affair, although for some days the life of the wounded man was despaired of. The perpetrator of the deed had not the slightest provocation from his unfortunate victim.

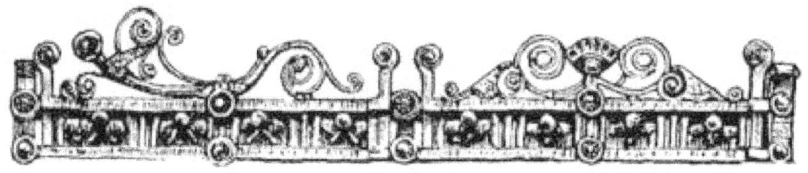

Letter the Fifteenth

[The Pioneer, May, 1855]

MINING METHODS—MINERS, GAMBLERS, ETC.

SYNOPSIS

Difficulty experienced in writing amid the charms of California mountain scenery. Science the blindest guide on a gold-hunting expedition. Irreverent contempt of the beautiful mineral to the dictates of science. Nothing better to be expected from the root of all evil. Foreigners more successful than Americans in its pursuit. Americans always longing for big strikes. Success lies in staying and persevering. How a camp springs into existence. Prospecting, panning out, and discovery that it pays. The claim. Building the shanty. Spreading of news of new diggings. Arrival of the monte-dealers. Industrious begin digging for gold. The claiming system. How claims worked. Working difficult amidst huge mountain rocks. Partnerships then compulsory. Naming the mine or company. The long-tom. Panning out the gold. Sinking shaft to reach bed-rock. Drifting coyote-holes in search of crevices. Water-ditches and water companies. Washing out in long-tom. Waste-ditches. Tailings. Fluming companies. Rockers. Gold-mining is nature's great lottery scheme. Thousands taken out in a few hours. Six ounces in six months. "Almost all seem to have lost". Jumped claims. Caving in of excavations. Abandonment of expensive paying shafts. Miner making "big strike" almost sure prey of professional gamblers. As spring opens, gamblers flock in like birds of prey. After stay of only four days, gambler leaves Bar with over a thousand dollars of miners' gold.

As many foreigners as Americans on the river. Foreigners generally extremely ignorant and degraded. Some Spaniards of the highest eduction and accomplishment. Majority of Americans mechanics of better class. Sailors and farmers next in number. A few merchants and steamboat-clerks. A few physicians. One lawyer. Ranchero of distinguished appearance an accomplished monte-dealer and horse-jockey. Said to have been a preacher in the States. Such not uncommon for California.

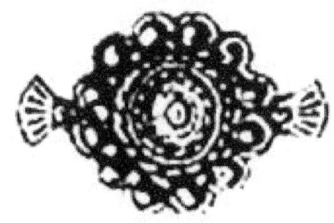

Letter the Fifteenth

Mining Methods—Miners, Gamblers, Etc.

From our Log Cabin, Indian Bar,

April 10, 1852.

I have been haunted all day, my dear M., with an intense ambition to write you a letter which shall be dreadfully commonplace and severely utilitarian in its style and contents. Not but that my epistles are *always* commonplace enough (spirits of Montague and Sévigné, forgive me!), but hitherto I have not really *tried* to make them so. Now, however, I *intend* to be stupidly prosy, with malice aforethought, and without one mitigating circumstance, except, perchance, it be the temptations of that above-mentioned ambitious little devil to palliate my crime.

You would certainly wonder, were you seated where I now am, how any one with a quarter of a soul *could* manufacture herself into a bore amid such surroundings as these. The air is as balmy as that of a midsummer's day in the sunniest valleys of New England. It is four o'clock in the evening, and I am sitting on a cigar-box outside of our cabin. From this spot not a person is to be seen, except a man who is building a new wing to the Humboldt. Not a human sound, but a slight noise made by the aforesaid individual in tacking on a roof of blue drilling to the room which he is finishing, disturbs the stillness which fills this purest air. I confess that it is difficult to fix my eyes upon the dull paper, and my fingers upon the duller pen with which I am soiling it. Almost every other minute I find myself stopping to listen to the ceaseless river-psalm, or to gaze up into the wondrous depths of the California heaven; to watch the graceful movements of the pretty brown lizards jerking up their impudent little heads above a moss-wrought log which lies before me, or to mark the dancing water-shadow on the canvas door of the bakeshop opposite; to follow with childish eyes the flight of a golden butterfly, curious to know if it will crown with a capital of winged beauty that column of nature's carving, the pine stump rising at my feet, or whether it will flutter down (for it is dallying coquettishly around them both) upon that slate-rock beyond, shining so darkly lustrous through a flood of yellow sunlight; or I lazily turn my head, wondering if I know the blue or red shirted miner who is descending the precipitous hill behind me. In sooth, Molly, it is easy to be commonplace at all times, but I confess that, just at present, I find it difficult to be utilitarian; the saucy lizards, the great orange-dotted butterflies, the still, solemn cedars, the sailing smoke-wreath, and the vaulted splendor above, are wooing me so winningly to higher things.

But, as I said before, I have an ambition that way, and I *will* succeed. You are such a good-natured little thing, dear, that I know you will meekly allow yourself to be victimized into reading the profound and prosy remarks which I shall make in my efforts to initiate you into the mining polity of this place. Now, you may rest assured that I shall assert nothing upon the subject which is not perfectly correct; for have I not earned a character for inquisitiveness (and you know that does *not* happen to be one of my failings) which I fear will cling to me through life, by my persevering questions to all the unhappy miners from whom I thought I could gain any information? Did I not martyrize myself into a human mule by descending to the bottom of a dreadful pit (suffering mortal terror all the time, lest it should cave in upon me), actuated by a virtuous desire to see with my own two eyes the process of underground mining, thus enabling myself to be stupidly correct in all my statements thereupon? Did I not ruin a pair of silk-velvet slippers, lame my ankles for a week, and draw a "browner horror" over my already sunburnt face, in a wearisome walk, miles away, to the head of the ditch, as they call the prettiest little rivulet (though the work of men) that I ever saw? Yea, verily, this have I done for the express edification of yourself and the rest of your curious tribe, to be rewarded, probably, by the impertinent remark, "What! *does* that little goose Dame Shirley think that *I* care about such things?" But, madam, in spite of your sneer, I shall proceed in my allotted task.

In the first place, then, as to the discovery of gold. In California, at least, it must be confessed that, in this particular, science appears to be completely at fault, or as an intelligent and well-educated miner remarked to us the other day, "I maintain that science is the blindest guide that one could have on a gold-finding expedition. Those men who judge by the appearance of the soil, and depend upon geological calculations, are invariably disappointed, while the ignorant adventurer, who digs just for the sake of digging, is almost sure to be successful." I suppose that the above observation is quite correct, as all whom we have questioned upon the subject repeat, in substance, the same thing. Wherever geology has said that *gold* must be, there, perversely enough, it lies not; and wherever her ladyship has declared that it could *not* be, there has it oftenest garnered up in miraculous profusion the yellow splendor of its virgin beauty. It is certainly very painful to a well-regulated mind to see the irreverent contempt shown by this beautiful mineral to the dictates of science. But what better can one expect from the root of all evil? As well as can be ascertained, the most lucky of the mining Columbuses have been ignorant sailors, and foreigners, I fancy, are more successful than Americans.

Our countrymen are the most discontented of mortals. They are always longing for big strikes. If a claim is paying them a steady income, by which, if they pleased, they could lay up more in a month than they could in a year at home, still they are dissatisfied, and in most cases will wander off in search of better diggings. There are hundreds now pursuing this foolish course, who, if they had stopped where they first camped, would now have been rich men. Sometimes a company of these wanderers will find itself upon a bar where a few pieces of the precious metal lie scattered upon the surface of the ground. Of course they immediately prospect it, which is accomplished by panning out a few basinfuls of the soil. If it pays, they claim the spot and build their shanties. The news spreads that wonderful diggings have been discovered at such a place. The monte-dealers—those worse than fiends—rush, vulture-like, upon the scene and erect a round tent, where, in gambling, drinking, swearing, and fighting, the *many* reproduce pandemonium in more than its original horror, while a *few* honestly and industriously commence digging for gold, and lo! as if a fairy's wand had been waved above the bar, a full-grown mining town hath sprung into existence.

But, first, let me explain to you the claiming system. As there are no state laws upon the subject, each mining community is permitted to make its own. Here they have decided that no man may claim an area of more than forty feet square. This he stakes off, and puts a notice upon it, to the effect that he holds it for mining purposes. If he does not choose to work it immediately, he is obliged to renew the notice every ten days, for, without this precaution, any other person has a right to "jump" it, that is, to take it from him. There are many ways of evading the above law. For instance, an individual can hold as many claims as he pleases if he keeps a man at work in each, for this workman represents the original owner. I am told, however, that the laborer himself can jump the claim of the very man who employs him, if he pleases so to do. This is seldom, if ever, done. The person who is willing to be hired generally prefers to receive the six dollars per diem, of which he is *sure* in any case, to running the risk of a claim not proving valuable. After all, the holding of claims by proxy is considered rather as a carrying out of the spirit of the law than as an evasion of it. But there are many ways of *really* outwitting this rule, though I cannot stop now to relate them, which give rise to innumerable arbitrations, and nearly every Sunday there is a miners' meeting connected with this subject.

Having got our gold-mines discovered and claimed, I will try to give you a faint idea of how they work them. Here, in the mountains, the labor of excavation is extremely difficult, on account of the immense rocks which form a large portion of the soil. Of course no man can work out a claim alone. For that reason, and also for the same that makes partnerships desirable, they congregate in companies of four or six, generally designating themselves by the name of the place from whence the majority of the members have emigrated; as, for example, the Illinois, Bunker Hill, Bay State, etc., companies. In many places the surface soil, or in mining phrase, the top dirt, pays when worked in a long-tom. This machine (I have never been able to discover the derivation of its name) is a trough, generally about twenty feet in length and eight inches in depth, formed of wood, with the exception of six feet at one end, called the "riddle" (query, why "riddle"?), which is made of sheet-iron perforated with holes about the size of a large marble. Underneath this colander-like portion of the long-tom is placed another trough, about ten feet long, the sides six inches, perhaps, in height, which, divided through the middle by a slender slat, is called the riffle-box. It takes several persons to manage properly a long-tom. Three or four men station themselves with spades at the head of the machine, while at the foot of it stands an individual armed "wid de shovel an' de hoe." The spadesmen throw in large quantities of the precious dirt, which is washed down to the riddle by a stream of water leading into the long-tom through wooden gutters or sluices. When the soil reaches the riddle, it is kept constantly in motion by the man with the hoe. Of course, by this means, all the dirt and gold escapes through the perforations into the riffle-box below, one compartment of which is placed just beyond the riddle. Most of the dirt washes over the sides of the riffle-box, but the gold, being so astonishingly heavy, remains safely at the bottom of it. When the machine gets too full of stones to be worked easily, the man whose business it is to attend to them throws them out with his shovel, looking carefully among them as he does so for any pieces of gold which may have been too large to pass through the holes of the riddle. I am sorry to say that he generally loses his labor. At night they pan out the gold which has been collected in the riffle-box during the day. Many of the miners decline washing the top dirt at all, but try to reach as quickly as possible the bed-rock, where are found the richest deposits of gold. The river is supposed to have formerly flowed over this bed-rock, in the crevices of which it left, as it passed away, the largest portions of the so eagerly sought for ore. The group of mountains amidst which we are living is a spur of the Sierra Nevada, and the bed-rock, which in this vicinity is of slate, is said to run through the entire range, lying, in distance varying from a few feet to eighty or ninety, beneath the surface of the soil. On Indian Bar the bed-rock falls in almost perpendicular benches, while at Rich Bar the friction of the river has formed it into large, deep basins, in which the gold, instead of being found, as you would naturally suppose, in the bottom of it, lies, for the most part, just below the rim. A good-natured individual bored *me*, and tired *himself,* in a hopeless attempt to make me comprehend that this was only a necessary consequence of the undercurrent of the water, but with my usual stupidity upon such matters I got but a vague idea from his scientific explanation, and certainly shall not mystify *you* with my confused notions thereupon.

When a company wish to reach the bed-rock as quickly as possible, they sink a shaft (which is nothing more nor less than digging a well) until they "strike it." They then commence drifting coyote-holes, as they call them, in search of crevices, which, as I told you before, often pay immensely. These coyote-holes sometimes extend hundreds of feet into the side of the hill. Of course they are obliged to use lights in working them. They generally proceed until the air is so impure as to extinguish the lights, when they return to the entrance of the excavation and commence another, perhaps close to it. When they think that a coyote-hole has been faithfully worked, they clean it up, which is done by scraping the surface of the bed-rock with a knife, lest by chance they have overlooked a crevice, and they are often richly rewarded for this precaution.

Now I must tell you how those having claims on the hills procure the water for washing them. The expense of raising it in any way from the river is too enormous to be thought of for a moment. In most cases it is brought from ravines in the mountains. A company, to which a friend of ours belongs, has dug a ditch about a foot in width and depth, and more than three miles in length, which is fed in this way. I wish that you could see this ditch. I never beheld a *natural* streamlet more exquisitely beautiful. It undulates over the mossy roots and the gray old rocks like a capricious snake, singing all the time a low song with the "liquidest murmur," and one might almost fancy it the airy and coquettish Undine herself. When it reaches the top of the hill, the sparkling thing is divided into five or six branches, each one of which supplies one, two, or three long-toms. There is an extra one, called the waste-ditch, leading to the river, into which the water is shut off at night and on Sundays. This race (another and peculiar name for it) has already cost the company more than five thousand dollars. They sell the water to others at the following rates. Those that have the first use of it pay ten per cent upon all the gold that they take out. As the water runs off from their machine (it now goes by the elegant name of "tailings"), it is taken by a company lower down, and as it is not worth so much as when it was clear, the latter pay but seven per cent. If any others wish the tailings, now still less valuable than at first, they pay four per cent on all the gold which they take out, be it much or little. The water companies are constantly in trouble, and the arbitrations on that subject are very frequent.

I think that I gave you a vague idea of fluming in a former letter. I will not, therefore, repeat it here, but will merely mention that the numerous fluming companies have already commenced their extensive operations upon the river.

As to the rockers, so often mentioned in story and in song, I have not spoken of them since I commenced this letter. The truth is, that I have seldom seen them used, though hundreds are lying ownerless along the banks of the river. I suppose that other machines are better adapted to mining operations in the mountains.

Gold-mining is nature's great lottery scheme. A man may work in a claim for many months, and be poorer at the end of the time than when he commenced, or he may take out thousands in a few hours. It is a mere matter of chance. A friend of ours, a young Spanish surgeon from Guatemala, a person of intelligence and education, told us that after working a claim for six months he had taken out but six ounces.

It must be acknowledged, however, that if a person work his claim himself, is economical and industrious, keeps his health, and is satisfied with small gains, he is bound to make money. And yet I cannot help remarking that almost all with whom we are acquainted seem to have *lost*. Some have had their claims jumped. Many holes, which had been excavated and prepared for working at a great expense, caved in during the heavy rains of the fall and winter. Often, after a company has spent an immense deal of time and money in sinking a shaft, the water from the springs (the greatest obstacle which the miner has to contend with in this vicinity) rushes in so fast that it is impossible to work in them, or to contrive any machinery to keep it out, and for that reason, only, men have been compelled to abandon places where they were at the very time taking out hundreds of dollars a day. If a fortunate or an unfortunate (which shall I call him?) *does* happen to make a big strike, he is almost sure to fall into the hands of the professed gamblers, who soon relieve him of all care of it. They have not troubled the Bar much during the winter, but as the spring opens they flock in like ominous birds of prey. Last week one left here, after a stay of four days, with over a thousand dollars of the hard-earned gold of the miners. But enough of these best-beloved of Beelzebub, so infinitely worse than the robber or murderer; for surely, it would be kinder to take a man's life than to poison him with the fatal passion for gambling.

Perhaps you would like to know what class of men is most numerous in the mines. As well as I can judge, there are upon this river as many foreigners as Americans. The former, with a few exceptions, are extremely ignorant and degraded, though we have the pleasure of being acquainted with three or four Spaniards of the highest education and accomplishments. Of the Americans, the majority are of the better class of mechanics. Next to these, in number, are the sailors and the farmers. There are a few merchants and steamboat-clerks, three or four physicians, and one lawyer. We have no ministers, though fourteen miles from here there is a rancho kept by a man of distinguished appearance, an accomplished monte-dealer and horse-jockey, who is *said* to have been, in the States, a preacher of the Gospel. I know not if this be true, but, at any rate, such things are not uncommon in California.

I have spun this letter out until my head aches dreadfully. How tiresome it is to write *sensible*(?) things! But I have one comfort: though my epistle may not be interesting, you will not deny, my dear M., that I have achieved my ambition of making it both commonplace and utilitarian.

Letter the Sixteenth

[The Pioneer, June, 1855]

BIRTH—STABBING—FOREIGNERS OUSTED—REVELS

SYNOPSIS

California mountain flora. A youthful Kanaka mother. Her feat of pedestrianism. Stabbing of a Spaniard by an American. The result of a request to pay a debt. Nothing done and but little said about the atrocity. Foreigners barred from working at Rich Bar. Spaniards thereupon move to Indian Bar. They erect places for the sale of intoxicants. Many new houses for public entertainment at Indian Bar. Sunday "swearing, drinking, gambling, and fighting". Salubrity of the climate. No death for months, except by accidental drowning in floodwater. Capture of grizzly cubs. "The oddest possible pets". "An echo from the outside world once a month."

Letter the Sixteenth
Birth—Stabbing—Foreigners Ousted—Revels
From our Log Cabin, Indian Bar,
May 1, 1852.

You have no idea, my good little M., how reluctantly I have seated myself to write to you. The truth is, that my last tedious letter about mining and other tiresome things has completely exhausted my scribbling powers, and from that hour to this the epistolary spirit has never moved me forward. Whether on that important occasion my small brain received a shock from which it will never recover, or whether it is pure physical laziness which influenced me, I know not; but this is certain, that no whipped schoolboy ever crept to his hated task more unwillingly than I to my writing-desk on this beautiful morning. Perhaps my indisposition to soil paper in your behalf is caused by the bewildering scent of that great, glorious bouquet of flowers which, gathered in the crisp mountain air, is throwing off cloud after cloud ("each cloud *faint* with the fragrance it bears") of languid sweetness, filling the dark old room with incense and making of it a temple of beauty, like those pure angelic souls which, irradiating a plain countenance, often render it more lovely than the chiseled finish of the most perfect features.

O Molly! how I wish that I could send you this jar of flowers, containing, as it does, many which, in New England, are rare exotics. Here you will find in richest profusion the fine-lady elegance of the syringa; there, glorious white lilies, so pure and stately; the delicate yet robust beauty of the exquisite privet; irises of every hue and size;

and, prettiest of all, a sweet snow-tinted flower, looking like immense clusters of seed-pearl, which the Spaniards call "libla." But the marvel of the group is an orange-colored blossom, of a most rare and singular fragrance, growing somewhat in the style of the flox. This, with some branches of pink bloom of incomparable sweetness, is entirely new to me. Since I have commenced writing, one of the Doctor's patients has brought me a bunch of wild roses. Oh, how vividly, at the sight of them, started up before me those wooded valleys of the Connecticut, with their wondrous depths of foliage, which, for a few weeks in midsummer, are perhaps unsurpassed in beauty by any in the world. I have arranged the dear *home* blossoms with a handful of flowers which were given to me this morning by an unknown Spaniard. They are shaped like an anemone, of the opaque whiteness of the magnolia, with a large spot of glittering blackness at the bottom of each petal. But enough of our mountain earth-stars. It would take me all day to describe their infinite variety.

Nothing of importance has happened since I last wrote, except that the Kanaka wife of a man living at The Junction has made him the happy father of a son and heir. They say that she is quite a pretty little woman, only fifteen years old, and walked all the way from Sacramento to this place.

A few evenings ago a Spaniard was stabbed by an American. It seems that the presumptuous foreigner had the impertinence to ask very humbly and meekly that most noble representative of the Stars and Stripes if the latter would pay him a few dollars which he had owed him for some time. His high mightiness the Yankee was not going to put up with any such impertinence, and the poor Spaniard received for answer several inches of cold steel in his breast, which inflicted a very dangerous wound. Nothing was done and very little was said about this atrocious affair.

At Rich Bar they have passed a set of resolutions for the guidance of the inhabitants during the summer, one of which is to the effect that no foreigner shall work in the mines on that bar. This has caused nearly all the Spaniards to immigrate upon Indian Bar, and several new houses for the sale of liquor, etc., are building by these people.

It seems to me that the above law is selfish, cruel, and narrow-minded in the extreme.

When I came here the Humboldt was the only public house on the Bar. Now there are the Oriental, Golden Gate, Don Juan, and four or five others, the names of which I do not know. On Sundays the swearing, drinking, gambling, and fighting which are carried on in some of these houses are truly horrible.

It is extremely healthy here. With the exception of two or three men who were drowned when the river was so high, I have not heard of a death for months.

Nothing worth wasting ink upon has occurred for some time, except the capture of two grizzly-bear cubs by the immortal Yank. He shot the mother, but she fell over the side of a steep hill and he lost her. Yank intends to tame one of the cubs. The other he sold, I believe for fifty dollars. They are certainly the funniest-looking things that I ever saw, and the oddest possible pets. By the way, we receive an echo from the outer world once a month, and the expressman never fails to bring three letters from my dear M. wherewith to gladden the heart of her sister, Dame Shirley.

Letter the Seventeenth
[The Pioneer, June, 1855]
SUPPLIES by PACK-MULES—KANAKAS and INDIANS
SYNOPSIS

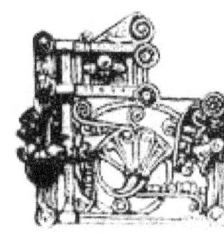

Belated arrival of pack-mule train with much-needed supplies. Picturesque appearance of the dainty-footed mules descending the hills. Of every possible color. Gay trappings. Tinkling bells. Peculiar urging cry of the Spanish muleteers. Lavish expenditure of gold-dust for vegetables and butter. Potatoes forty cents a pound. Incense of the pungent member of the lily family. Arrival of other storm-bound trains, and sudden collapse in prices. Horseback ride on dangerous trail. Fall of oxen over precipice. Mountain flowers, oaks, and rivulets. Visit to Kanaka mother. A beauty from the isles. Hawaiian superstition. An unfortunate request for the baby as a present. Consolatory promise to give the next one. Indian visitors. Head-dresses. "Very tight and very short shirts". Indian mode of life. Their huts, food, cooking, utensils, manner of eating. Sabine-like invasion leaves to tribe but a few old squaws. "Startlingly unsophisticated state of almost entire nudity". Their filthy habits. Papooses fastened in framework of light wood. Indian modes of fishing. A handsome but shy young buck. Classic gracefulness of folds of white-sheet robe of Indian. Light and airy step of the Indians something superhuman. Miserably brutish and degraded. Their vocabulary Of about twenty words. Their love of gambling, and its frightful consequences. Arrival of hundreds of people at Indian Bar.

Saloons springing up in every direction. Fluming operations rapidly progressing. A busy, prosperous summer looked for.

Letter the Seventeenth

Supplies by Pack-Mules—Kanakas and Indians

From our Log Cabin, Indian Bar,

May 25, 1852.

The very day after I last wrote you, dear M., a troop of mules came onto the Bar, bringing us almost-forgotten luxuries, in the form of potatoes, onions, and butter. A band of these animals is always a pretty sight, and you can imagine that the solemn fact of our having been destitute of the above-mentioned edibles since the middle of February did not detract from the pleasure with which we saw them winding cautiously down the hill, stepping daintily here and there with those absurd little feet of theirs, and appearing so extremely anxious for the safe conveyance of their loads. They belonged to a Spanish packer, were in excellent condition, sleek and fat as so many kittens, and of every possible color,—black, white, gray, sorrel, cream, brown, etc. Almost all of them had some bit of red or blue or yellow about their trappings, which added not a little to the brilliancy of their appearance; while the gay tinkle of the leader's bell, mingling with those shrill and peculiar exclamations with which Spanish muleteers are in the habit of urging on their animals, made a not unpleasing medley of sounds. But the creamiest part of the whole affair was—I must confess it, unromantic as it may seem—when the twenty-five or thirty pretty creatures were collected into the small space between our cabin and the Humboldt. Such a gathering together of ham-and-mackerel-fed bipeds, such a lavish display of gold-dust, such troops of happy-looking men bending beneath the delicious weight of butter and potatoes, and, above all, *such* a smell of fried onions as instantaneously rose upon the fragrant California air and ascended gratefully into the blue California heaven was, I think, never experienced before.

On the 1st of May a train had arrived at Rich Bar, and on the morning of the day which I have been describing to you one of our friends arose some three hours earlier than usual, went over to the aforesaid bar, bought twenty-five pounds of potatoes at forty cents a pound, and packed them home on his back. In less than two days afterwards half a dozen cargoes had arrived, and the same vegetable was selling at a shilling a pound. The trains had been on the road several weeks, but the heavy showers, which had continued almost daily through the month of April, had retarded their arrival.

Last week I rode on horseback to a beautiful bar called The Junction, so named from the fact that at that point the East Branch of the North Fork of Feather River unites itself with the main North Fork. The mule-trail, which lies along the verge of a dreadful precipice, is three or four miles long, while the footpath leading by the river is not more than two miles in length. The latter is impassable, on account of the log bridges having been swept away by the recent freshets. The other day two oxen lost their footing and fell over the precipice, and it is the general opinion that they were killed long before they reached the golden palace of the Plumerian Thetis. I was a little alarmed at first, for fear my horse would stumble, in which case I should have shared the fate of the unhappy beeves, but soon forgot all fear in the enchanting display of flowers which each opening in the shrubs displayed to me. Earth's firmament was starred with daphnes, irises, and violets of every hue and size; pale wood-anemones, with but one faint sigh of fragrance as they expired, died by hundreds beneath my horse's tread; and spotted tiger-lilies, with their stately heads all bedizened in orange and black, marshaled along the path like an army of gayly clad warriors. But the flowers are not all of an oriental character. Do you remember, Molly dear, how you and I once quarreled when we were, oh, such mites of children, about a sprig of syringa? The dear mother was obliged to interfere, and to make all right she gave you a small brown bud, of most penetrating fragrance, which she told you was much more valuable than the contested flower. I remember perfectly that she failed entirely in convincing me *that* the dark, somber flower was half as beautiful as my pretty cream-tinted blossom, and, if I mistake not, you were but poutingly satisfied with the substitute. Here, even if we retained, which I do not, our childish fascination for syringas, we should not need to quarrel about them, for they are as common as dandelions in a New England meadow, and dispense their peculiar perfume—which, by the way, always reminds me of Lubin's choicest scents—in almost sickening profusion. Besides the above-mentioned flowers, we saw wild roses and buttercups and flox and privet, and whole acres of the wand-like lily. I have often heard it said, though I cannot vouch for the truth of the assertion, that it is only during the month of January that you cannot gather a bouquet in the mountains.

Just before one reaches The Junction there is a beautiful grove of oaks, through which there leaps a gay little rivulet celebrated for the grateful coolness of its waters. Of course one is expected to propitiate this pretty Undine by drinking a draft of her glittering waters from a dirty tin cup which some benevolent cold-water man has suspended from a tree near the spring. The bank leading down into the stream is so steep that people generally dismount and lead their animals across it, but F. declared that I was so light that the horse could easily carry me, and insisted upon my keeping the saddle. Of course, like a dutiful wife, I had nothing to do but to obey. So I grasped firmly the reins, shut my eyes, and committed myself to the Fates that take care of thistle-seeds, and lo! the next moment I found myself safely on the other side of the brook, my pretty steed—six weeks ago he was an Indian pony running wild on the prairie—curveting about and arching his elegant neck, evidently immensely proud of the grace and ease with which he had conveyed his burden across the brook. In a few moments we alighted at the store, which is owned by some friends of F., whom we found looking like so many great daisies in their new shirts of pink calico, which had been donned in honor of our expected arrival.

The Junction is the most beautiful of all the bars. From the store one can walk nearly a mile down the river quite easily. The path is bordered by a row of mingled oaks and firs, the former garlanded with mistletoe, and the latter embroidered with that exquisitely beautiful moss which I tried to describe in one of my first letters.

The little Kanaka woman lives here. I went to see her. She is quite pretty, with large lustrous eyes, and two great braids of hair which made me think of black satin cables, they were so heavy and massive. She has good teeth, a sweet smile, and a skin not much darker than that of a French brunette. I never saw any creature so proud as she, almost a child herself, was of her baby. In jest, I asked her to give it to me, and really was almost alarmed at the vehement burst of tears with which she responded to my request. Her husband explained the cause of her distress. It is a superstition among her people that he who refuses to give another anything, no matter what,—there are no exceptions which that other may ask for,—will be overwhelmed with the most dreadful misfortunes. Her own parents had parted with her for the same reason. Her pretty girlish face soon resumed its smiles when I told her that I was in jest, and, to console me for the disappointment which she thought I must feel at not obtaining her little brown treasure, she promised to give me the *next* one! It is a Kanaka custom to make a present to the person calling upon them for the first time, in accordance with which habit I received a pair of dove-colored boots three sizes too large for me.

I should have liked to visit the Indian encampment which lies a few miles from The Junction, but was too much fatigued to attempt it. The Indians often visit us, and as they seldom wear anything but a *very* tight and *very* short shirt, they have an appearance of being, as Charles Dickens would say, all legs. They usually sport some kind of a head-dress, if it is nothing more than a leather string, which they bind across their dusky brows in the style of the wreaths in Norma, or the gay ribbons garlanding the hair of the Roman youth in the play of Brutus. A friend of ours, who has visited their camp several times, has just given me a description of their mode of life. Their huts, ten or twelve in number, are formed of the bark of the pine, conically shaped, plastered with mud, and with a hole in the top, whence emerges the smoke, which rises from a fire built in the center of the apartment. These places are so low that it is quite impossible to stand upright in them, and are entered from a small hole in one side, on all fours. A large stone, sunk to its surface in the ground, which contains three or four pan-like hollows for the purpose of grinding acorns and nuts, is the only furniture which these huts contain. The women, with another stone, about a foot and a half in length and a little larger than a man's wrist, pulverize the acorns to the finest possible powder, which they prepare for the table(?) in the following manner. Their cooking utensils consist of a kind of basket, woven of some particular species of reed, I should fancy, from the descriptions which I have had of them, and are so plaited as to be impervious to fluids. These they fill half full of water, which is made to boil by placing in it hot stones. The latter they drag from the fire with two sticks. When the water boils, they stir into it, until it is about as thick as hasty-pudding, the powdered acorns, delicately flavored with dried grasshoppers, and lo! dinner is ready. Would you like to know how they eat? They place the thumb and little finger together across the palm of the hand, and make of the other three fingers a spoon, with which they shovel into their capacious mouths this delicious compound.

There are about eighty Indians in all at this encampment, a very small portion of which number are women. A hostile tribe in the valley made a Sabine-like invasion upon the settlement a few months since, and stole away all the young and fair muchachas, leaving them but a few old squaws. These poor withered creatures, who are seldom seen far from the encampment, do all the drudgery. Their entire wardrobe consists of a fringe about two feet in length, which is formed of the branch or root—I cannot ascertain exactly which—of a peculiar species of shrub shredded into threads. This scanty costume they festoon several times about the person, fastening it just above the hips, and they generally appear in a startlingly unsophisticated state of almost entire nudity. They are very filthy in their habits, and my informant said that if one of them should venture out into the rain, grass would grow on her neck and arms. The men, unhappy martyrs! are compelled to be a little more cleanly, from their custom of hunting and fishing, for the wind *will* blow off *some* of the dirt, and the water washes off more.

Their infants are fastened to a framework of light wood, in the same manner as those of the North American Indians. When a squaw has anything to do, she very composedly sets this frame up against the side of the house as a civilized housewife would an umbrella or broom.

Some of their modes of fishing are very curious. One is as follows. These primitive anglers will seek a quiet deep spot in the river, where they know fish most do congregate, and throw therein a large quantity of stones. This, of course, frightens the fish, which dive to the bottom of the stream, and Mr. Indian, plunging head foremost into the water, beneath which he sometimes remains several minutes, will presently reappear, holding triumphantly in each hand one of the finny tribe, which he kills by giving it a single bite in the head or neck with his sharp, knife-like teeth.

Hardly a day passes during which there are not three or four of them on this Bar. They often come into the cabin, and I never order them away, as most others do, for their childish curiosity amuses me, and as yet they have not been troublesome. There is one beautiful little boy, about eight years old, who generally accompanies them. We call him Wild Bird, for he is as shy as a partridge, and we have never yet been able to coax him into the cabin. He always wears a large red shirt, which, trailing to his little bronzed feet, and the sleeves every other minute dropping down over his dusky models of hands, gives him a very odd appearance. One day Mrs. B., whom I was visiting at the time, coaxed Wild Bird into the house to see Charley, the hero of the champagne-basket cradle. The little fellow gazed at us with his large, startled eyes without showing the least shadow of fear in his countenance, but his heart beat so violently that we could actually see the rise and fall of the old red shirt which covered its tremblings. Mrs. B. made our copper-colored Cupidon a pretty suit of crimson calico. His protectors—half a dozen grim old Indians (it was impossible to tell which was his father, they all made such a petted darling of him)—were compelled to array him in his new suit by main strength, he screaming dreadfully all the time. Indeed, so exhausted was he by his shrieks that by the time he was fairly buttoned up in his crimson trappings he sank on the ground in a deep sleep. The next day the barbarous little villain appeared trailing, as usual, his pet shirt after him at every step, while the dandy jacket and the trim baby-trousers had vanished we never knew whither.

The other morning an Indian appeared on the Bar robed from neck to heels in a large white sheet, and you have no idea of the classic grace with which he had arranged the folds about his fine person. We at first thought him a woman, and he himself was in an ecstasy of glee at our mistake.

It is impossible to conceive of anything more light and airy than the step of these people. I shall never forget with what enchanted eyes I gazed upon one of them gliding along the side of the hill opposite Missouri Bar. One would fancy that nothing but a fly or a spirit could keep its footing on the rocks along which he stepped so stately, for they looked as perpendicular as a wall. My friend observed that no white man could have done it. This wild creature seemed to move as a cloud moves on a quiet day in summer, and as still and silently. It really made me solemn to gaze upon him, and the sight almost impressed me as something superhuman.

Viewed in the most favorable manner, these poor creatures are miserably brutish and degraded, having very little in common with the lofty and eloquent aborigines of the United States. It is said that their entire language contains but about twenty words. Like all Indians, they are passionately fond of gambling, and will exhibit as much anxiety at the losing or winning of a handful of beans as do their paler brothers when thousands are at stake. Methinks, from what I have seen of that most hateful vice, the *amount* lost or won has very little to do with the matter. But let me not speak of this most detestable of crimes. I have known such frightful consequences to ensue from its indulgence, that I dare not speak of it, lest I use language, as perhaps I have already done, unbecoming a woman's lips.

Hundreds of people have arrived upon our Bar within the last few days; drinking-saloons are springing up in every direction; the fluming operations are rapidly progressing; and all looks favorably for a busy and prosperous summer to our industrious miners.

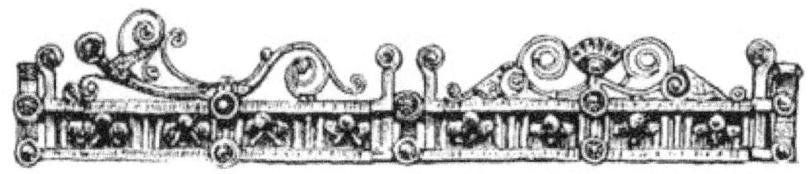

Letter the Eighteenth

[The Pioneer, July, 1852]

FOURTH of JULY FESTIVAL—SPANISH ATTACKED

SYNOPSIS

Fourth of July celebration at Rich Bar. The author makes the flag. Its materials. How California was represented therein. Floated from the top of a lofty pine. The decorations at the Empire Hotel. An "officious Goth" mars the floral piece designed for the orator of the day. Only two ladies in the audience. Two others expected, but do not arrive. No copy of the Declaration of Independence. Preliminary speeches by political aspirants. Orator of the day reads anonymous poem. Oration "exceedingly fresh and new". Belated arrival of the expected ladies, new-comers from the East. With new fashions, they extinguish the author and her companion. Dinner at the Empire. Mexican War captain as president. "Toasts quite spicy and original". Fight in the barroom. Eastern lady "chose to go faint" at sight of blood. Cabin full of "infant phenomena". A rarity in the mountains. Miners, on way home from celebration, give nine cheers for mother and children. Outcry at Indian Bar against Spaniards. Several severely wounded. Whisky and patriotism. Prejudices and arrogant assurance accounted for. Misinterpretation by the foreigner. Injustices by the lower classes against Spaniards pass unnoticed. Innumerable drunken fights. Broken heads and collarbones, stabbings. "Sabbaths almost always enlivened by such merry events". Body of Frenchman found in river. Murder evident. Suspicion falls on nobody.

Letter the Eighteenth
Fourth of July Festival—Spanish Attacked
From our Log Cabin, Indian Bar,
July 5, 1852.

Our Fourth of July celebration, dear M., which came off at Rich Bar, was quite a respectable affair. I had the honor of making a flag for the occasion. The stripes were formed of cotton cloth and red calico, of which last gorgeous material no possible place in California is ever destitute. A piece of drilling, taken from the roof of the Humboldt, which the rain and the sun had faded from its original somber hue to just that particular shade of blue which you and I admire so much, served for a union. A large star in the center, covered with gold-leaf, represented California. Humble as were the materials of which it was composed, this banner made quite a gay appearance floating from the top of a lofty pine in front of the Empire, to which it was suspended.

I went over to Rich Bar at six in the morning, not wishing to take so fatiguing a walk in the heat of the day. After breakfast I assisted Mrs. B. and one of the gentlemen in decorating the dining-room, the walls of which we completely covered with grape-vines, relieved here and there with bunches of elder-blow. We made several handsome bouquets, and arranged one of syringas, white lilies, and the feathery green of the cedar, to be presented, in the name of the ladies, to the orator of the day. You can imagine my disgust, when the ceremony was performed, to observe that some officious Goth had marred the perfect keeping of the gift by thrusting into the vase several ugly purple blossoms.

The exercises were appointed to commence at ten o'clock, but they were deferred for half an hour, in expectation of the arrival of two ladies who had taken up their abode in the place within the last six weeks, and were living on Indian Bar hill. As they did not come, however, it was thought necessary to proceed without them. So Mrs. B. and myself were obliged to sit upon the piazza of the Empire, comprising, in our two persons, the entire female audience.

The scene was indeed striking. The green-garlanded hills girdling Rich Bar looked wonderfully beautiful, rising with their grand abrupt outlines into the radiant summer sky. A platform reared in front of the Empire, beneath the banner-tasseled pine, and arched with fragrant fir boughs, made the prettiest possible rustic rostrum. The audience, grouped beneath the awnings of the different shops, dressed in their colored shirts,—though here and there one might observe a dandy miner who had relieved the usual vestment by placing beneath it one of calico or white muslin,—added much to the picturesqueness of the scene. Unfortunately, the committee of arrangements had not been able to procure a copy of the Declaration of Independence. Its place was supplied by an apologetic speech from a Mr. J., who will, without doubt, be the Democratic candidate for state representative at the coming election. This gentleman finished his performance by introducing Mr. B., the orator of the day, who is the Whig nominee for the above-mentioned office. Before pronouncing his address, Mr. B. read some verses which he said had been handed to him anonymously the evening before. I have copied them for your amusement. They are as follows, and are entitled—

A FOURTH of JULY WELCOME to the MINERS

Ye are welcome, merry miners, in your blue and red shirts all;
Ye are welcome, 'mid these golden hills, to your nation's festival;
Though ye've not shaved your savage lips nor cut your barb'rous hair,
Ye are welcome, merry miners, all bearded as ye are.

What though your brows are blushing at the kisses of the sun,
And your once white and well-kept hands are stained a sober dun;
What though your backs are bent with toil, and ye have lost the air
With which ye bowed your stately heads amid the young and fair,

I fain would in my slender palm your horny fingers clasp,
For I love the hand of honest toil, its firm and heartfelt grasp;
And I know, O miners brave and true, that not alone for self
Have ye heaped, through many wearying months, your glittering
pile of pelf.

Ye of the dark and thoughtful eyes beneath the bronzèd brow,
Ye on whose smooth and rounded cheeks still gleams youth's purple
glow,
Ye of the reckless, daring life, ye of the timid glance;
Ho! young and old; ho! grave and gay,—to our nation's fête
advance.

Ho! sun-kissed brother from the South, where radiant skies are
glowing;
Ho! toiler from the stormy North, where snowy winds are blowing;
Ho! Buckeye, Hoosier, from the West, sons of the river great,—
Come, shout Columbia's birthday song in the new Golden State.

Ho! children of imperial France; ho! Erin's brave and true;
Ho! England's golden-bearded race,—we fain would welcome you,
And dark-eyed friends from those glad climes where Spain's proud
blood is seen;
To join in Freedom's holy psalm ye'll not refuse, I ween.

For now the banner of the free's in *very deed* our own,
And, 'mid the brotherhood of states, not ours the feeblest one.
Then proudly shout, ye bushy men with throats all brown and bare,

For, lo! from 'midst our flag's brave blue, leaps out a *golden* star.

After reading the above lines, Mr. B. pronounced beautifully a very splendid oration. Unlike such efforts in general, it was exceedingly fresh and new, so that, instead of its being that infliction that Fourth of July orations commonly are, it was a high pleasure to listen to him. Perhaps, where nature herself is so original, it is impossible for even thought to be hackneyed. It is too long for a letter, but as the miners have requested a copy for publication, I will send it to you in print.

About half an hour after the close of the oration the ladies from the hill arrived. They made a pretty picture descending the steep,—the one with her wealth of floating curls turbaned in a snowy nubia, and her white dress set off by a crimson scarf; the other with a little Pamela hat placed coquettishly upon her brown braided tresses, and a magnificent Chinese shawl enveloping her slender figure. So lately arrived from the States, with everything fresh and new, they quite extinguished poor Mrs. B. and myself, trying our best to look fashionable in our antique mode of four years ago.

The dinner was excellent. We had a real live captain, a very gentlemanly person, who had actually been in action during the Mexican War, for president. Many of the toasts were quite spicy and original; one of the new ladies sang three or four beautiful songs; and everything passed off at Rich Bar quite respectably. To be sure, there was a small fight in the barroom, which is situated just below the dining-room, during which much speech and a little blood were spouted. Whether the latter catastrophe was caused by a blow received, or the large talking of the victim, is not known. Two peacefully inclined citizens, who at the first battle-shout had rushed manfully to the rescue, returned at the subsiding of hostilities with blood-bespattered shirt-bosoms, at which fearful sight the pretty wearer of the Pamela hat—one of the delinquents being her husband—chose to go faint, and would not finish her dinner, which, as we saw that her distress was real, somewhat marred our enjoyment.

On our way home, half a dozen gentlemen who preceded us stepped in front of a cabin full of infant phenomena and gave nine cheers for the mother and her children; which will show what a rarity those embodiments of noise and disquiet are in the mountains. This group of pretty darlings consists of three sweet little girls, slender, straight, and white as ivory wands, moving with an incessant and staccato (do you remember our old music lessons?) activity which always makes me think of my hummingbirds.

About five o'clock we arrived at home, just in time to hear some noisy shouts of "Down with the Spaniards," "The great American people forever," and other similar cries, evident signs of quite a spirited fight between the two parties, which was, in reality, taking place at the moment. Seven or eight of the élite of Rich Bar, drunk with whisky and patriotism, were the principal actors in this unhappy affair, which resulted in serious injury to two or three Spaniards. For some time past there has been a gradually increasing state of bad feeling exhibited by our countrymen (increased, we fancy, by the ill-treatment which our consul received the other day at Acapulco) towards foreigners. In this affair our own countrymen were principally to blame, or, rather, I should say, Sir Barleycorn was to blame, for many of the ringleaders are fine young men who, when sober, are decidedly friendly to the Spaniards. It is feared that this will not be the end of the fracas, though the more intelligent foreigners, as well as the judicious Americans, are making every effort to promote kindly feeling between the two nations. This will be very difficult, on account of the ignorant prejudices of the low-bred, which class are a large proportion of both parties.

It is very common to hear vulgar Yankees say of the Spaniards, "O, they are half-civilized black men!" These unjust expressions naturally irritate the latter, many of whom are highly educated gentlemen of the most refined and cultivated manners. We labor under great disadvantages, in the judgment of foreigners. Our peculiar political institutions, and the prevalence of common schools, give to *all* our people an arrogant assurance which is mistaken for the American beau-ideal of a gentleman.

They are unable to distinguish those nice *shades* of manner which as effectually separate the gentleman from the clown with *us* as do these broader lines which mark these two classes among all other nations. They think that it is the grand characteristic of Columbia's children to be prejudiced, opinionated, selfish, avaricious, and unjust. It is vain to tell them that such are not specimens of American gentlemen. They will answer, "They call themselves gentlemen, and you receive them in your houses as such." It is utterly impossible for foreigners to thoroughly comprehend and make due allowance for that want of delicacy, and that vulgar "I'm as good as you are" spirit, which is, it must be confessed, peculiar to the lower classes of our people, and which would lead the majority of them to—

Enter a palace with their old felt hat on;
To address the King with the title of Mister,
And ask him the price of the throne he sat on.

The class of men who rule society(?) in the mines are the gamblers, who, for the most part, are reckless, bad men, although, no doubt, there are many among them whose only vice is that fatal love of play. The rest of the people are afraid of these daring, unprincipled persons, and when they commit the most glaring injustice against the Spaniards, it is generally passed unnoticed.

We have had innumerable drunken fights during the summer, with the usual amount of broken heads, collar-bones, stabs, etc. Indeed, the sabbaths are almost always enlivened by some such merry event. Were it not for these affairs, I might sometimes forget that the sweet day of rest was shining down upon us.

Last week the dead body of a Frenchman was found in the river, near Missouri Bar. On examination of the body it was the general opinion that he had been murdered. Suspicion has, as yet, fallen upon no person.

Letter the Nineteenth

[The Pioneer, August, 1855]

MURDER, THEFT, RIOT, HANGING, WHIPPING, ETC.

SYNOPSIS

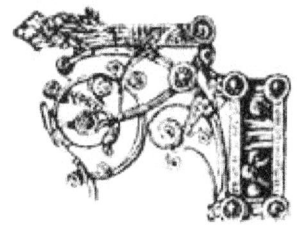

Three weeks of excitement at Indian Bar. Murders, fearful accidents, bloody deaths, whippings, hanging, attempted suicide, etc. A sabbath-morning walk in the hills. Miners' ditch rivaling in beauty the work of nature. Fatal stabbing by a Spaniard. Afterwards parades street with a Mexicana, brandishing a long bloody knife. His pursuit by and escape from the infuriated Americans. Unfounded rumor of conspiracy of Spaniards to murder Americans. Spaniards barricade themselves. Grief of Spanish woman over corpse of murdered man. Miners arrive from Rich Bar. Wild cry for vengeance, and for expulsion of Spaniards. The author prevailed upon to retire to place of safety. Accidental discharge of gun when drunken owner of vile resort attempts to force way through armed guard. Two seriously wounded. Sobering effect of the accident. Vigilance committee organized. Suspected Spaniards arrested. Trial of the Mexicana. Always wore male attire, was foremost in fray, and, armed with brace of pistols, fought like a fury. Sentenced to leave by daylight. Indirect cause of fight. Woman always to blame. Trial of ringleaders. Sentences of whipping, and to leave. Confiscation of property for benefit of wounded. Anguish of the author when Spaniards were whipped. Young Spaniard movingly but vainly pleads for death instead of whipping. His oath to murder every American he should afterwards meet alone. Doubtless will keep his word. Murder of Mr. Bacon, a ranchero, for his money, by his negro cook. Murderer caught at Sacramento with part of money. His trial at Rich Bar by the vigilantes. Sentence of death by hanging. Another negro attempts suicide. Accuses mulatto Ned of attempt to murder him. Dr. C. in trouble for binding up negro's self-inflicted wounds. Formation of "Moguls," who make night hideous. Vigilantes do not interfere. Duel at Missouri Bar. Fatal results. A large crowd present. Vigilance committee also present. "But you must remember that this is California."

Letter the Nineteenth
Murder, Theft, Riot, Hanging, Whipping, &c.
From our Log Cabin, Indian Bar,
August 4, 1852.

 We have lived through so much of excitement for the last three weeks, dear M., that I almost shrink from relating the gloomy events that have marked their flight. But if I leave out the darker shades of our mountain life, the picture will be very incomplete. In the short space of twenty-four days we have had murders, fearful accidents, bloody deaths, a mob, whippings, a hanging, an attempt at suicide, and a fatal duel. But to begin at the beginning, as, according to rule, one ought to do.

I think that, even among these beautiful hills, I never saw a more perfect bridal of the earth and sky than that of Sunday, the 11th of July. On that morning I went with a party of friends to the head of the ditch, a walk of about three miles in length. I do not believe that nature herself ever made anything so lovely as this artificial brooklet. It glides like a living thing through the very heart of the forest, sometimes creeping softly on, as though with muffled feet, through a wilderness of aquatic plants, sometimes dancing gayly over a white-pebbled bottom, now making a sunshine in a shady place, across the mossy roots of the majestic old trees, and anon leaping with a grand anthem adown the great solemn rocks which lie along its beautiful pathway. A sunny opening at the head of the ditch is a garden of perfumed shrubbery and many-tinted flowers, all garlanded with the prettiest vines imaginable, and peopled with an infinite variety of magnificent butterflies. These last were of every possible color, pink, blue and yellow, shining black splashed with orange, purple flashed with gold, white, and even green. We returned about three in the evening, loaded with fragrant bundles, which, arranged in jars, tumblers, pitchers, bottles, and pails, (we are not particular as to the quality of our vases in the mountains, and love our flowers as well in their humble chalices as if their beautiful heads lay against a background of marble or porcelain,) made the dark old cabin a bower of beauty for us.

Shortly after our arrival, a perfectly deafening volley of shouts and yells elicited from my companion the careless remark that the customary sabbath-day's fight was apparently more serious than usual. Almost as he spoke there succeeded a deathlike silence, broken in a minute after by a deep groan at the corner of the cabin, followed by the words, "Why, Tom, poor fellow, are you really wounded?" Before we could reach the door, it was burst violently open by a person who inquired hurriedly for the Doctor, who, luckily, happened at that very moment to be approaching. The man who called him then gave us the following excited account of what had happened. He said that in a mêlée between the Americans and the foreigners, Domingo, a tall, majestic-looking Spaniard, a perfect type of the novelistic bandit of Old Spain, had stabbed Tom Somers, a young Irishman, but a naturalized citizen of the United States, and that, at the very moment, said Domingo, with a Mexicana hanging upon his arm, and brandishing threateningly the long, bloody knife with which he had inflicted the wound upon his victim, was parading up and down the street unmolested. It seems that when Tom Somers fell the Americans, being unarmed, were seized with a sudden panic and fled. There was a rumor (unfounded, as it afterwards proved) to the effect that the Spaniards had on this day conspired to kill all the Americans on the river. In a few moments, however, the latter rallied and made a rush at the murderer, who immediately plunged into the river and swam across to Missouri Bar. Eight or ten shots were fired at him while in the water, not one of which hit him. He ran like an antelope across the flat, swam thence to Smith's Bar, and escaped by the road leading out of the mountains from The Junction. Several men went in pursuit of him, but he was not taken, and without doubt is now safe in Mexico.

In the mean while the consternation was terrific. The Spaniards, who, with the exception of six or eight, knew no more of the affair than I did, thought that the Americans had arisen against them, and our own countrymen, equally ignorant, fancied the same of the foreigners. About twenty of the latter, who were either sleeping or reading in their cabins at the time of the *émeute*, aroused by the cry of "Down with the Spaniards!" barricaded themselves in a drinking-saloon, determined to defend themselves as long as possible against the massacre which was fully expected would follow this appalling shout. In the bakeshop, which stands next door to our cabin, young Tom Somers lay straightened for the grave (he lived but fifteen minutes after he was wounded), while over his dead body a Spanish woman was weeping and moaning in the most piteous and heartrending manner. The Rich Barians, who had heard a most exaggerated account of the rising of the Spaniards against the Americans, armed with rifles, pistols, clubs, dirks, etc., were rushing down the hill by hundreds. Each one added fuel to his rage by crowding into the little bakery to gaze upon the blood-bathed bosom of the victim, yet warm with the life which but an hour before it had so triumphantly worn. Then arose the most fearful shouts of "Down with the Spaniards!" "Drive every foreigner off the river!" "Don't let one of the murderous devils remain!" "Oh, if you have a drop of American blood in your veins, it must cry out for vengeance upon the cowardly assassins of poor Tom!" All this, mingled with the most horrible oaths and execrations, yelled up as if in mockery into that smiling heaven, which, in its fair sabbath calm, bent unmoved over the hell which was raging below.

After a time the more sensible and sober part of the community succeeded in quieting, in a partial degree, the enraged and excited multitude. During the whole affair I had remained perfectly calm,— in truth, much more so than I am now, when recalling it. The entire catastrophe had been so unexpected, and so sudden in its consummation, that I fancy I was stupefied into the most exemplary good behavior. F. and several of his friends, taking advantage of the lull in the storm, came into the cabin and entreated me to join the two women who were living on the hill. At this time it seemed to be the general opinion that there would be a serious fight, and they said I might be wounded accidentally if I remained on the Bar. As I had no fear of anything of the kind, I pleaded hard to be allowed to stop, but when told that my presence would increase the anxiety of our friends, of course, like a dutiful wife, I went on to the hill.

We three women, left entirely alone, seated ourselves upon a log overlooking the strange scene below. The Bar was a sea of heads, bristling with guns, rifles, and clubs. We could see nothing, but fancied from the apparent quiet of the crowd that the miners were taking measures to investigate the sad event of the day. All at once we were startled by the firing of a gun, and the next moment, the crowd dispersing, we saw a man led into the log cabin, while another was carried, apparently lifeless, into a Spanish drinking-saloon, from one end of which were burst off instantly several boards, evidently to give air to the wounded person. Of course we were utterly unable to imagine what had happened, and, to all our perplexity and anxiety, one of the ladies insisted upon believing that it was her own husband who had been shot, and as she is a very nervous woman, you can fancy our distress. It was in vain to tell her—which we did over and over again—that that worthy individual wore a *blue* shirt, and the wounded person a *red* one. She doggedly insisted that her dear M. had been shot, and, having informed us confidentially, and rather inconsistently, that she should never see him again, never, never, plumped herself down upon the log in an attitude of calm and ladylike despair, which would have been infinitely amusing had not the occasion been so truly a fearful one. Luckily for our nerves, a benevolent individual, taking pity upon our loneliness, came and told us what had happened.

It seems that an Englishman, the owner of a house of the vilest description, a person who is said to have been the primary cause of all the troubles of the day, attempted to force his way through the line of armed men which had been formed at each side of the street. The guard very properly refused to let him pass. In his drunken fury he tried to wrest a gun from one of them, which, being accidentally discharged in the struggle, inflicted a severe wound upon a Mr. Oxley, and shattered in the most dreadful manner the thigh of Señor Pizarro, a man of high birth and breeding, a porteño of Buenos Aires. This frightful accident recalled the people to their senses, and they began to act a little less like madmen than they had previously done. They elected a vigilance committee, and authorized persons to go to The Junction and arrest the suspected Spaniards.

The first act of the committee was to try a Mexicana who had been foremost in the fray. She has always worn male attire, and upon this occasion, armed with a pair of pistols, she fought like a very fury. Luckily, inexperienced in the use of firearms, she wounded no one. She was sentenced to leave the Bar by daylight,—a perfectly just decision, for there is no doubt that she is a regular little demon. Some went so far as to say she ought to be hanged, for she was the *indirect* cause of the fight. You see, always it is the old cowardly excuse of Adam in Paradise,—the woman *tempted* me, and I did eat,—as if the poor frail head, once so pure and beautiful, had not sin enough of its own, dragging it forever downward, without being made to answer for the wrong-doing of a whole community of men.

The next day the committee tried five or six Spaniards, who were proven to have been the ringleaders in the sabbath-day riot. Two of them were sentenced to be whipped, the remainder to leave the Bar that evening, the property of all to be confiscated to the use of the wounded persons. O Mary! imagine my anguish when I heard the first blow fall upon those wretched men. I had never thought that I should be compelled to hear such fearful sounds, and, although I immediately buried my head in a shawl, nothing can efface from memory the disgust and horror of that moment. I had heard of such things, but heretofore had not realized that in the nineteenth century men could be beaten like dogs, much less that other men not only could sentence such barbarism, but could actually stand by and see their own manhood degraded in such disgraceful manner. One of these unhappy persons was a very gentlemanly young Spaniard, who implored for death in the most moving terms. He appealed to his judges in the most eloquent manner, as gentlemen, as men of honor, representing to them that to be deprived of life was nothing in comparison with the never-to-be-effaced stain of the vilest convict's punishment to which they had sentenced him. Finding all his entreaties disregarded, he swore a most solemn oath, that he would murder every American that he should chance to meet alone, and as he is a man of the most dauntless courage, and rendered desperate by a burning sense of disgrace which will cease only with his life, he will doubtless keep his word.

Although, in my very humble opinion, and in that of others more competent to judge of such matters than myself, these sentences were unnecessarily severe, yet so great was the rage and excitement of the crowd that the vigilance committee could do no less. The mass of the mob demanded fiercely the death of the prisoners, and it was evident that many of the committee took side with the people. I shall never forget how horror-struck I was (bombastic as it *now* sounds) at hearing no less a personage than the Whig candidate for representative say that the condemned had better fly for their lives, for the "Avenger of Blood" was on their tracks! I am happy to say that said very worthy but sanguinary individual, the Avenger of Blood, represented in this case by some half-dozen gambling rowdies, either changed his mind or lost scent of his prey, for the intended victims slept about two miles up the hill quite peacefully until morning.

The following facts, elicited upon the trial, throw light upon this unhappy affair. Seven miners from Old Spain, enraged at the cruel treatment which their countrymen had received on the Fourth, and at the illiberal cry of "Down with the Spaniards," had united for the purpose of taking revenge on seven Americans, whom they believed to be the originators of their insults. All well armed, they came from The Junction, where they were residing at the time, intending to challenge each one his man, and in fair fight compel their insolent aggressors to answer for the arrogance which they had exhibited more than once towards the Spanish race. Their first move, on arriving at Indian Bar, was to go and dine at the Humboldt, where they drank a most enormous quantity of champagne and claret. Afterwards they proceeded to the house of the Englishman whose brutal carelessness caused the accident which wounded Pizarro and Oxley, when one of them commenced a playful conversation with one of his countrywomen. This enraged the Englishman, who instantly struck the Spaniard a violent blow and ejected him from the shanty. Thereupon ensued a spirited fight, which, through the exertion of a gentleman from Chile, a favorite with both nations, ended without bloodshed. This person knew nothing of the intended duel, or he might have prevented, by his wise counsels, what followed. Not suspecting for a moment anything of the kind, he went to Rich Bar. Soon after he left, Tom Somers, who is said always to have been a dangerous person when in liquor, without any apparent provocation struck Domingo (one of the original seven) a violent blow, which nearly felled him to the earth. The latter, a man of "dark antecedents" and the most reckless character, mad with wine, rage, and revenge, without an instant's pause drew his knife and inflicted a fatal wound upon his insulter. Thereupon followed the chapter of accidents which I have related.

On Tuesday following the fatal sabbath, a man brought news of the murder of a Mr. Bacon, a person well known on the river, who kept a ranch about twelve miles from Rich Bar. He was killed for his money by his servant, a negro, who, not three months ago, was our own cook. He was the last one anybody would have suspected capable of such an act.

A party of men, appointed by the vigilance committee, left the Bar immediately in search of him. The miserable wretch was apprehended in Sacramento, and part of the gold found upon his person. On the following Sunday he was brought in chains to Rich Bar. After a trial by the miners, he was sentenced to be hanged at four o' clock in the evening. All efforts to make him confess proved futile. He said very truly that whether innocent or guilty they would hang him, and so he "died and made no sign" with a calm indifference, as the novelists say, worthy of a better cause. The dreadful crime and death of Josh, who, having been an excellent cook, and very neat and respectful, was a favorite servant with us, added to the unhappiness which you can easily imagine that I was suffering under all these horrors.

On Saturday evening, about eight o'clock, as we sat quietly conversing with the two ladies from the hill,—whom, by the way, we found very agreeable additions to our society, hitherto composed entirely of gentlemen,—we were startled by the loud shouting, and the rushing close by the door of the cabin, which stood open, of three or four hundred men. Of course we feminines, with nerves somewhat shattered from the events of the past week, were greatly alarmed.

We were soon informed that Henry Cook, vice Josh, had, in a fit of delirium tremens, cut his throat from ear to ear. The poor wretch was alone when he committed the desperate deed, and in his madness, throwing the bloody razor upon the ground, ran part of the way up the hill. Here he was found almost senseless, and brought back to the Humboldt, where he was very nearly the cause of hanging poor Paganini Ned, who returned a few weeks since from the valley; for his first act on recovering himself was to accuse that culinary individual of having attempted to murder him.

The mob were for hanging one poor Vattel without judge or jury, and it was only through the most strenuous exertions of his friends that the life of this illustrious person was saved. Poor Ned! It was forty-eight hours before his corkscrews returned to their original graceful curl. He threatens to leave us to our barbarism, and no longer to waste his culinary talents upon an ungrateful and inappreciative people. He has sworn war to the knife against Henry, who was formerly his most intimate friend, as nothing can persuade him that the accusation did not proceed from the purest malice on the part of the would-be suicide.

Their majesties the mob, with that beautiful consistency which usually distinguishes those august individuals, insisted upon shooting poor Harry, for, said they,—and the reasoning is remarkably conclusive and clear,—a man so hardened as to raise his hand against his *own* life will never hesitate to murder another! They almost mobbed F. for binding up the wounds of the unfortunate wretch, and for saying that it was possible he might live. At last, however, they compromised the matter by determining that if Henry should recover he should leave the Bar immediately. Neither contingency will probably take place, as it will be almost a miracle if he survives.

On the day following the attempted suicide, which was Sunday, nothing more exciting happened than a fight and the half-drowning of a drunken individual in the river, just in front of the Humboldt.

On Sunday last the thigh of Señor Pizarro was amputated, but, alas! without success. He had been sick for many months with chronic dysentery, which, after the operation, returned with great violence, and he died at two o'clock on Monday morning, with the same calm and lofty resignation which had distinguished him during his illness. When first wounded, believing his case hopeless, he had decidedly refused to submit to amputation, but as time wore on he was persuaded to take this one chance for his life for the sake of his daughter, a young girl of fifteen, at present at school in a convent in Chile, whom his death leaves without any near relative. I saw him several times during his illness, and it was melancholy indeed to hear him talk of his motherless girl, who, I have been told, is extremely beautiful, talented, and accomplished.

The state of society here has never been so bad as since the appointment of a committee of vigilance. The rowdies have formed themselves into a company called the "Moguls," and they parade the streets all night, howling, shouting, breaking into houses, taking wearied miners out of their beds and throwing them into the river, and, in short, "murdering sleep" in the most remorseless manner. Nearly every night they build bonfires fearfully near some rag shanty, thus endangering the lives (or, I should rather say, the property, for, as it is impossible to sleep, lives are emphatically safe) of the whole community. They retire about five o'clock in the morning, previously to this blessed event posting notices to that effect, and that they will throw any one who may disturb them into the river. I am nearly worn out for want of rest, for, truly, they "make night hideous" with their fearful uproar.

Mr. Oxley, who still lies dangerously ill from the wound received on what we call the "fatal Sunday," complains bitterly of the disturbances; and when poor Pizarro was dying, and one of his friends gently requested that they be quiet for half an hour and permit the soul of the sufferer to pass in peace, they only laughed and yelled and hooted louder than ever in the presence of the departing spirit, for the tenement in which he lay, being composed of green boughs only, could, of course, shut out no sounds.

Without doubt, if the Moguls had been sober, they would never have been guilty of such horrible barbarity as to compel the thoughts of a dying man to mingle with curses and blasphemies, but, alas! they were intoxicated, and may God forgive them, unhappy ones, for they knew not what they did. The poor, exhausted miners—for even well people cannot sleep in such a pandemonium—grumble and complain, but they, although far outnumbering the rioters, are too timid to resist. All say, "It is shameful," "Something ought to be done," "Something *must* be done," etc., and in the mean time the rioters triumph; You will wonder that the committee of vigilance does not interfere. It is said that some of that very committee are the ringleaders among the Moguls.

I believe I have related to you everything but the duel, and I will make the recital of this as short as possible, for I am sick of these sad subjects, and doubt not but you are the same. It took place on Tuesday morning, at eight o'clock, on Missouri Bar, when and where that same Englishman who has figured so largely in my letter shot his best friend. The duelists were surrounded by a large crowd, I have been told, foremost among which stood the committee of vigilance!

The man who received his dear friend's fatal shot was one of the most quiet and peaceable citizens on the Bar. He lived about ten minutes after he was wounded. He was from Ipswich, England, and only twenty-five years old when his own high passions snatched him from life. In justice to his opponent it must be said that he would willingly have retired after the first shots had been exchanged, but poor Billy Leggett, as he was familiarly called, insisted upon having the distance between them shortened, and continuing the duel until one of them had fallen.

There, my dear M., have I not fulfilled my promise of giving you a dish of horrors? And only think of such a shrinking, timid, frail thing as I *used* to be "long time ago" not only living right in the midst of them, but almost compelled to hear, if not see, the whole. I think I may without vanity affirm that I have "seen the elephant." "Did you see his tail?" asks innocent Ada J., in her mother's letter. Yes, sweet Ada; the entire animal has been exhibited to my view. "But you must remember that this is California," as the new-comers are so fond of informing *us*! who consider ourselves "one of the oldest inhabitants" of the Golden State.

And now, dear M., adios. Be thankful that you are living in the beautiful quiet of beautiful A., and give up "hankering arter" (as you know what dear creature says) California, for, believe me, this coarse, barbarous life would suit you even less than it does your sister.

Letter the Twentieth
[The Pioneer, September, 1855]
MURDER—MINING SCENES—SPANISH BREAKFAST
SYNOPSIS

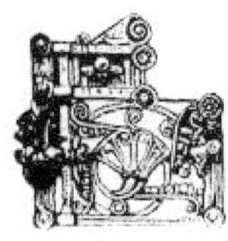

Ramada, unoccupied, wrecked by log rolling down hill. Was place of residence of wounded Spaniard, who died but a few days previously. Murder near Indian Bar. Innocent and harmless person arrested, said to answer description of murderer. A humorous situation. A "guard of honor" from the vigilantes while in custody. Upon release his expenses paid. Had a rest from hard work. Tendered a present and a handsome apology. Public opinion in the mines a cruel but fortunately a fickle thing. Invitation to author to breakfast at Spanish garden. The journey thereto, along river, with its busy mining scenes. The wing-dam, and how it differs from the ordinary dam. An involuntary bath. Drifts, shafts, coyote-holes. How claims are worked. Flumes. Unskilled workmen. Their former professions or occupations. The best water in California, but the author is unappreciative. Flavorless, but, since the Flood, always tastes of sinners. Don Juan's country-seat. The Spanish breakfast. The eatables and the drinkables. Stronger spirits for the stronger spirits. Ice, through oversight, the only thing lacking. Yank's tame cub. Parodic doggerel by the author on her loss of pets. A miners' dinner-party with but one teaspoon, and that one borrowed. An unlearned and wearisome blacksmith.

Letter the Twentieth

Murder—Mining Scenes—Spanish Breakfast

From our Log Cabin, Indian Bar,

September 4, 1852.

If I could coax some good-natured fairy or some mischievous Puck to borrow for me the pen of Grace Greenwood, Fanny Forester, or Nathaniel P. Willis, I might be able to weave my stupid nothings into one of those airy fabrics the value of which depends entirely upon the skillful work, or rather penmanship, which distinguishes it. I have even fancied that if I could steal a feather from the living opal swinging like a jeweled pendulum from the heart of the great tiger-lily which nods its turbaned head so stately within the mosquito-net cage standing upon the little table, my poor lines would gather a certain beauty from the rainbow-tinted quill with which I might trace them. But as there is nobody magician enough to go out and shoot a fairy or a brownie and bind it by sign and spell to do my bidding, and as I have strong doubts whether my coarse fingers would be able to manage the delicate pen of a humming-bird even if I could have the heart to rob my only remaining pet of its brilliant feathers, I am fain to be content with one of "Gillott's Best,"—no, of "C. R. Sheton's Extra Fine," although I am certain that the sentences following its hard stroke will be as stiff as itself. If they were only as bright, one might put up with the want of grace, but to be stiff and stupid both, is *too* provoking, is it not, dear M.? However, what must be, must be;

and as I have nothing to write about, and do not possess the skill to make that nothing graceful, and as you will fret yourself into a scold if you do not receive the usual amount of inked pages at the usual time, why, of course I am bound to act (my first appearance on *any* stage, I flatter myself in *that* character) the very original part of the *bore*, and you must prepare to be bored with what philosophy you may.

But, without further preface, I will begin with one of the nothings. A few days after the death of the unfortunate Spaniard, related in my last letter, a large log, felled by some wickedly careless woodman, rolled down from one of the hills, and so completely extinguished the little ramada in which our poor friend lay at the time of his death that you would never have imagined from the heap of broken branches that remain that it had once been a local habitation with such a pretty name. Providentially, at the time of the accident, none of those who had been in the habit of staying there were within. If Señor Pizarro had survived the amputation of his leg, it would only have been to suffer a still more terrible death,—an accident which would have deepened, if possible, the gloom which we have suffered during the melancholy summer.

There has been another murder committed within a few miles of this place, which has given us something to gossip about, for the committee of vigilance had the good nature, purely for our amusement I conclude, to apprehend a lucky individual (I call him *lucky* advisedly, for he had all his expenses paid at the Humboldt, was remunerated for his lost time, enjoyed a holiday from hard work, had a sort of guard of honor composed of the most respectable men on the river, and was of more consequence for four days than ever he had been in the whole of his insignificant little life before) whom somebody fancied bore a faint resemblance to the description of the murderer. This interesting lion—I was so fortunate as to catch a glimpse of him one morning, and am convinced that he would "roar you as gently as any sucking dove"—was fully cleared from the suspected crime; and if, before his acquittal, one might have fancied from the descriptions of his countenance that none but that of Mephistopheles in the celebrated picture of the Game of Life could equal its terrific malignity, after-accounts drew it a very Saint John's for sweet serenity of expression. What was then called sullenness now took the name of resignation, and stupidity was quiet contempt. Indeed, I began to fear that they would give him a public triumph, and invite me to make the flag with which to grace it. I confess that I would almost have voted him a procession myself, in gratitude for the amusement which he had given us. However, the committee were content with making him a handsome apology and present, and paying his expenses at the Humboldt. O public opinion in the mines, thou art in truth a *cruel* thing, but, thank God, most *fickle*!

The other day we were invited by a Spanish friend to breakfast at a garden situated half a mile from The Junction, and owned by another Spaniard. It was a lovely morning in the latter part of August, and as we started about six o'clock, the walk was a most delightful one. The river, filled with flumes, dams, etc., and crowded with busy miners, was as much altered from its old appearance as if an earthquake had frightened it from its propriety.

I suppose that you are quite worn out with descriptions of walks, and I will spare you this once. I will not tell you how sometimes we were stepping lightly over immense rocks which a few months since lay fathoms deep beneath the foaming Plumas; nor how sometimes we were walking high above the bed of the river, from flume to flume, across a board connecting the two; nor how now we were scrambling over the roots of the upturned trees, and now jumping tiny rivulets; nor shall I say a single word about the dizziness we felt as we crept by the deep excavations lying along the road, nor of the beautiful walk at the side of the wing-dam (it differs from a common dam, in dividing the river lengthways instead of across), the glittering water rising bluely almost to a level with the path. I do not think that I will ever tell you about the impromptu bath which one of the party took by tumbling accidentally into the river as he was walking gallantly behind us, which said bath made him decidedly disagree in our enthusiastic opinion of the loveliness of the promenade.

No; I shall not say a single word upon any of these subjects, but leave them all to your vivid imagination. Corkscrews could not draw a solitary sentence from me, now that I have made up my mind to silence. But I *will* tell you about the driftings in the side of the hill, which we visited on our way,—not so much from a precious desire of enlightening your pitiable ignorance upon such subjects, you poor, little, untraveled Yankee woman! but to prove to you that, having fathomed the depths of shafts, and threaded the mazes of coyote-holes, I intend to astonish the weak nerves of stay-at-homes, if I ever return to New England, by talking learnedly upon such subjects, as one having authority.

These particular "claims" consist of three galleries lying about eighty feet beneath the summit of the hill, and have already been drifted from one hundred and fifty to two hundred feet into its side. They are about five feet in height, slightly arched, the sides and roof, formed of rugged rocks, dripping with moisture, as if sweating beneath the great weight above. Lights are placed at regular distances along these galleries to assist the miners in their work, and boards laid on the wet ground to make a convenient path for the wheelbarrows which convey the dirt and sand to the river for the purpose of washing it. Wooden beams are placed here and there to lessen the danger of caving in, but I must confess that in spite of this precaution I was at first haunted with a horrible feeling of insecurity. As I became reassured I repeated loudly those glorious lines of Mrs. Hemans commencing with—

> For the strength of the hills we bless thee,
> O God, our fathers' God!

And a strange echo the gray rocks sent back, as if the mine-demons, those ugly gnomes which German legends tell us work forever in the bowels of the earth, were shouting my words in mockery from the dim depths beyond.

These claims have paid remarkably well, and if they hold out as they have commenced, the owners will gather a small fortune from their summer's work.

There is nothing which impresses me more strangely than the fluming operations. The idea of a mighty river being taken up in a wooden trough, turned from the old channel along which it has foamed for centuries perhaps, its bed excavated many feet in depth, and itself restored to its old home in the fall,—these things strike me as almost a blasphemy against nature, And then the idea of men succeeding in such a work here in the mountains, with machinery and tools of the poorest description, to say nothing of the unskilled workmen,—doctors, lawyers, ministers, scholars, gentlemen, farmers, etc.

When we arrived at the little oak-opening described in a former letter, we were, of course, in duty bound to take a draft from the spring, which its admirers declare is the best water in all California. When it came to my turn, I complacently touched the rusty tin cup, though I never *did* care much for water, in the abstract, *as* water. Though I think it very useful to make coffee, tea, chocolate, and other good drinks, I could never detect any other flavor in it than that of *cold*, and have often wondered whether there was any truth in the remark of a character in some play, that, ever since the world was drowned in it, it had tasted of sinners!

When we arrived at what may be called, in reference to the Bar, the country-seat of Don Juan, we were ushered into the parlor, two sides of which opened upon the garden and the grand old mountains which rise behind it, while the other two sides and the roof were woven with fresh willow boughs, crisply green, and looking as if the dew had scarcely yet dried from the polished leaves.

After opening some cans of peaches, and cutting up some watermelons gathered from the garden, our friends went in to, or rather *out* to, the kitchen fire (two or three stones are generally the extent of this useful apartment in the mines) to assist in preparing the breakfast—and *such* a breakfast! If "Tadger could do it when it chose," so can we miners. We had—but what did we *not* have? There were oysters which, I am sure, could not have been nicer had they just slid from their shells on the shore at Amboy; salmon, in color like the red, red gold; venison with a fragrant spicy gusto, as if it had been fed on cedar-buds; beef cooked in the Spanish fashion,—that is, strung onto a skewer and roasted on the coals,—than which I never tasted better; preserved chicken; and almost every possible vegetable bringing up the rear. Then, for drinkables, we had tea, coffee, and chocolate; champagne, claret, and porter, with stronger spirits *for* the stronger spirits. We lacked but one thing. That was ice; which we forgot to bring from the Bar. As, only four miles from our cabin, the snow never melts, that is a luxury we are never without, and, indeed, so excessively warm has been the season, that without it, and the milk which has been brought us daily from a rancho five miles from here, we should have suffered. I must say that even though we had no ice, our mountain picnic, with its attendant dandies in their blue and red flannel shirts, was the most charming affair of the kind that I ever attended.

On our return we called to see Yank's cub, which is fast rising into young grizzly-bearhood. It is about the size of a calf, very good-natured, and quite tame. Its acquirements, as yet, are few, being limited to climbing a pole. Its education has not been conducted with that care and attention which so intelligent a beast merits, but it is soon, I hear, to be removed to the valley and placed under teachers capable of developing its wonderful talents to the utmost.

We also stopped at a shanty to get a large gray squirrel which had been promised to me some days before; but I certainly am the most unfortunate wretch in the world with pets. This spiteful thing, on purpose to annoy me I do believe, went and got itself drowned the very night before I was to take it home. It is always so.

> I never had two humming-birds,
> With plumage like a sunset sky,
> But one was sure to fly away,
> And the other one was sure to die.
>
> I never nursed a flying-squirrel,
> To glad me with its soft black eye,
> But it always ran into somebody's tent,
> Got mistaken for a rat and killed!

There, M.; there is poetry for you. "Oh, the second verse doesn't rhyme."—"Doesn't?"—"And it ain't original, is it?" Well, *I* never heard that rhyme was necessary to make a poet, any more than colors to make a painter. And what if Moore *did* say the same thing twenty years ago? I am sure any writer would consider himself lucky to have an idea which has been anticipated but *once*. I am tired of being a "mute inglorious Milton," and, like that grand old master of English song, would gladly write something which the world would not willingly let die; and having made that first step, as witness the above verses, who knows what will follow?

Last night one of our neighbors had a dinner-party. He came in to borrow a teaspoon. "Had you not better take them all?" I said. "Oh, no," was the answer; "that would be too much luxury. My guests are not used to it, and they would think that I was getting aristocratic, and putting on airs. One is enough; they can pass it round from one to the other."

A blacksmith—not the learned one—has just entered, inquiring for the Doctor, who is not in, and he is obliged to wait. Shall I write down the conversation with which he is at this moment entertaining me? "Who writ this 'ere?" is his first remark, taking up one of my most precious books, and leaving the marks of his irreverent fingers upon the clean pages. "Shakespeare," I answer, as politely as possible. "Did Spokeshave write it? He was an almighty smart fellow, that Spokeshave, I've hear'n tell," replies my visitor. "I must write hum and tell our folks that this 'ere is the first carpet I've seen sin' I came to Californy, four year come next month," is his next remark. For the last half-hour he has been entertaining me with a wearisome account of the murder of his brother by an Irishman in Boston, and the chief feeling which he exhibits is a fear that the jury should only bring in a verdict of manslaughter. But I hear F.'s step, and his entrance relieves me from the bore.

I am too tired to write more. Alas, dear M. this letter is indeed a stupid one—a poor return for your pregnant epistles. It is too late to better it. The express goes at eight in the morning. The midnight moon is looking wonderingly in at the cabin window, and the river has a sleepy murmur that impels me irresistibly bedward.

Letter the Twenty-first

[The Pioneer, October, 1855]

DISCOMFORTS of TRIP to POLITICAL CONVENTION

SYNOPSIS

Visit to the American Valley. Journey thither. Scenes by the way. Political convention. Delegates from Indian Bar. Arrival at Greenwood's Rancho, headquarters of Democrats. Overcrowded. Party proceed to the American Rancho, headquarters of Whigs. Also overcrowded. Tiresome ride of ladies on horseback. Proceed to house of friend of lady in party. An inhospitable reception, but the author entertains herself. Men of party return to American Rancho. Inroad upon the eatables. Landlord aghast, but pacified by generous orders for drinkables. California houses not proof against eavesdroppers. Misunderstandings and explanations overheard by the author. Illness of hostess. Uncomfortable and miserable night, and worse quarters. Handsome riding-habit, etc., of the hostess. Table-service, carpeting, chests of tea, casks of sugar, bags of coffee, etc., "the good people possessed everything but a house". "The most beautiful spot I ever saw in California". Owner building house of huge hewn logs. The author returns to the American Rancho. Its primitive furniture, etc. Political visitors. The convention. Horse-racing and gambling. The author goes to Greenwood's Rancho. More primitive furniture and lack of accommodations. Misplaced benevolence of Bostonians. Should transfer their activities to California.

Letter the Twenty-first
Discomforts of Trip to Political Convention
From our Log Cabin, Indian Bar,
October 16, 1852.

Since I last wrote you, dear M., I have spent three weeks in the American Valley, and I returned therefrom humbled to the very dust when thinking of my former vainglorious boast of having "seen the elephant." To be sure, if having fathomed to its very depths the power of mere existence, without any reference to those conventional aids which civilization has the folly to think necessary to the performance of that agreeable duty, was any criterion, I certainly fancied that I had a right to brag of having taken a full view of that most piquant specimen of the brute creation, the California "elephant." But it seems that I was mistaken, and that we miners have been dwelling in perfect palaces, surrounded by furniture of the most gorgeous description, and reveling in every possible luxury. Well, one lives and learns, even on the borders of civilization. But to begin at the beginning, let me tell you the history of my dreadful pleasure-tour to the American Valley.

You must know that a convention had been appointed to meet at that place for the purpose of nominating representatives for the coming election. As F. had the misfortune to be one of the delegates, nothing would do but I must accompany him; for, as my health had really suffered through the excitements of the summer, he fancied that change of air might do me good. Mrs. ——, one of our new ladies, had been invited to spend a few weeks in the same place, at the residence of a friend of her husband, who was living there with his family. As Mr. —— was also one of the delegates, we made up a party together, and, being joined by two or three other gentlemen, formed quite a gay cavalcade.

The day was beautiful. But when is it ever otherwise in the mountains of California? We left the Bar by another ascent than the one from which I entered the Bar, and it was so infinitely less steep than the latter, that it seemed a mere nothing. You, however, would have fancied it quite a respectably hill, and Mr. —— said that so fearful did it seem to him the first time he went down it, that he vowed never to cross it but once more,—a vow, by the way, which has been broken many times. The whole road was a succession of charming tableaux, in which sparkling streamlets, tiny waterfalls, frisky squirrels gleaming amid the foliage like a flash of red light, quails with their pretty gray plumage flecked with ivory, dandy jays, great awkward black crows, pert little lizards, innumerable butterflies, and a hundred other

> Plumèd insects, winged and free,
> Like golden boats on a sunny sea,

were the characters, grouped in a frame of living green, curtained with the blue folds of our inimitable sky.

We had intended to start very early in the morning, but, as usual on such excursions, did not get off until about ten o'clock. Somebody's horse came up missing, or somebody's saddle needed repairing, or somebody's shirt did not come home in season from the washer-Chinaman (for if we *do* wear flannel shirts, we choose to have them clean when we ride out with the ladies), or something else equally important detained us. It was about nine o'clock in the evening when we reached the valley and rode up to Greenwood's Rancho, which, by the way, was the headquarters of the Democratic party. It was crowded to overflowing, as our ears told us long before we came in sight of it, and we found it utterly impossible to obtain lodgings there. This building has no windows, but a strip of crimson calico, placed half-way from the roof and running all round the house, lets in the *red* light and supplies their place. However, we did not stop long to enjoy the pictorial effect of the scarlet windows,—which really look very prettily in the night,—but rode straight to the American Rancho, a quarter of a mile beyond. This was the headquarters of the Whigs, to which party our entire company, excepting myself, belonged. Indeed, the gentlemen had only consented to call at the other house through compassion for the ladies, who were suffering from extreme fatigue, and they were rejoiced at the prospect of getting among birds of the same feather. There, however, we were informed that it was equally impossible to procure accommodations. In this dilemma we could do nothing but accept Mrs. ———'s kind invitation and accompany her to the rancho of her friend, although she herself had intended, as it was so late, to stop at one of the hotels for the night. We were so lucky as to procure a guide at this place, and with this desirable addition to the party, we started on.

I had been very sick for the last two hours, and had only kept up with the thought that we should soon arrive at our journey's end; but when I found that we were compelled to ride three miles farther, my heart sank within me. I gave up all attempts to guide my horse, which one of the party led, leaned my head on the horn of my saddle, and resigned myself to my fate. We were obliged to walk our horses the entire distance, as I was too sick to endure any other motion. We lost our way once or twice, were exhausted with fatigue and faint with hunger, chilled through with the cold, and our feet wet with the damp night-air.

I forgot to tell you that Mrs. ———, being very fleshy, was compelled to ride astride, as it would have been utterly impossible for her to have kept her seat if she had attempted to cross those steep hills in the usual feminine mode of sitting a horse. She wore dark-gray bloomers, and, with a Kossuth hat and feather, looked like a handsome chubby boy. Now, riding astride, to one unaccustomed to it, is, as you can easily imagine, more safe than comfortable, and poor Mrs. ——— was utterly exhausted.

When we arrived at our destined haven, which we did at last, the gentleman of the house came forward and invited Mr. and Mrs. ——— to alight. Not a word was said to the rest of us, not even "Good evening." But I was too far gone to stand upon ceremony. So I dismounted and made a rush for the cooking-stove, which, in company with an immense dining-table on which lay (enchanting sight!) a quarter of beef, stood under a roof, the four sides open to the winds of heaven. As for the remainder of the party, they saw how the land lay, and vamosed to parts unknown, namely, the American Rancho, where they arrived at four o'clock in the morning, some tired, I *guess*, and made such a fearful inroad upon the eatables that the proprietor stood aghast, and was only pacified by the ordering in from the bar of a most generous supply of the drinkable, which, as he sells it by the glass, somewhat reconciled him to the terrific onslaught upon the larder.

In the mean time behold me, with much more truth than poetry literally alone in my glory, seated upon a wooden stool, with both feet perched upon the stove, and crouching over the fire in a vain attempt to coax some warmth into my thoroughly chilled frame. The gentleman and lady of the house, with Mr. and Mrs. ——, are assembled in grand conclave, in one room, of which the building consists, and as California houses are *not* planned with a view to eavesdroppers, I have the pleasure of hearing the following spirited and highly interesting conversation. There is a touching simplicity about it truly dramatic.

I must premise that Mrs. —— had written the day before to know if the visit, which her husband's friend had so earnestly solicited, would be conveniently received at this time, and was answered by the arrival, the next morning, for the use of herself and husband, of two horses, one of which I myself had the pleasure of riding, and found it a most excellent steed. Moreover, when Mr. —— gave her the invitation, he said he would be pleased to have one of her lady friends accompany her. So you see she was "armed and equipped as the law directed."

Thus defended, she was ushered into the presence of her hostess, whom she found reclining gracefully upon a very nice bed hung with snow-white muslin curtains, looking—for she is extremely pretty, though now somewhat pale—like a handsome wax doll.

"I am extremely sorry to find you unwell. Pray, when were you taken? and are you suffering much at present?" commenced Mrs. ———, supposing that her illness was merely an attack of headache, or some other temporary sickness.

"Ah," groaned my lady, in a faint voice, "I have had a fever, and am just beginning to get a little better. I have not been able to sit up any yet, but hope to do so in a few days. As we have no servants, my husband is obliged to nurse me, as well as to cook for several men, and I am really afraid that, under the circumstances, you will not be as comfortable here as I could wish."

"But, good heavens, my dear madam, why did you not send me word that you were sick? Surely you must have known that it would be more agreeable to me to visit you when you are in health," replied Mrs. ———.

"Oh," returned our fair invalid, "I thought that you had set your heart upon coming, and would be disappointed if I postponed the visit."

Now, this was adding insult to injury. Poor Mrs. ———! Worn out with hunger, shivering with cold, herself far from well, a new-comer, unused to the makeshift ways which some people fancy essential to California life, expecting from the husband's representations—and knowing that he was very rich—so different a reception, and withal frank perhaps to a fault, she must be pardoned if she was not as grateful as she ought to have been, and answered a little crossly,—

"Well, I must say that I have not been treated well. Did you really think that I was so childishly crazy to get away from home that I would leave my nice plank house,"—it rose into palatial splendor when compared with the floorless shanty, less comfortable than a Yankee farmer's barn, in which she was standing,—"with its noble fireplace, nice board floor, two pleasant windows, and comfortable bed, for this wretched place? Upon my word, I am very much disappointed. However, I do not care so much for myself as for poor Mrs. ———, whom I persuaded to come with me."

"What! is there *another* lady?" almost shrieked (and well she might, under the circumstances) the horror-stricken hostess. "You can sleep with me, but I am sure I do not know what we can do with another one."

"Certainly," was the bold reply of Mrs. ——, for she was too much provoked to be embarrassed in the least. "Availing myself of your husband's kind permission, I invited Mrs. ——, who could not procure lodgings at either of the hotels, to accompany me. But even if I were alone I should decidedly object to sleep with a sick person, and should infinitely prefer wrapping myself in my shawl and lying on the ground to being guilty of such a piece of selfishness."

"Well," groaned the poor woman, "Jonathan" (or Ichabod, or David, or whatever was the domestic name of her better half), "I suppose that you must make up some kind of a bed for them on the ground."

Now, M., only fancy my hearing all this! *Wasn't* it a fix for a sensitive person to be in? But, instead of bursting into tears and making myself miserable, as once I should have done, I enjoyed the contretemps immensely. It almost cured my headache, and when Mrs. —— came to me and tried to soften matters, I told her to spare her pretty speeches, as I had heard the whole and would not have missed it for anything.

In the mean time the useful little man, combining in his small person the four functions of husband, cook, nurse, and gentleman, made us a cup of tea and some saleratus biscuit, and though I detest saleratus biscuit, and was longing for some of the beef, yet, by killing the taste of the alkali with onions, we contrived to satisfy our hunger, and the tea warmed us a little. Our host, in his capacity of chambermaid, had prepared us a couch. I was ushered into the presence of the fair invalid, to whom I made a polite apology for my intrusion. My feet sank nearly to the ankles in the dirt and small stones as I walked across her room.

But how shall I describe to you the sufferings of that dreadful night? I have slept on tables, on doors, and on trunks. I have reclined on couches, on chairs, and on the floor. I have lain on beds of straw, of corn-husks, of palm-leaf, and of ox-hide. I remember one awful night spent in a bedbuggy berth, on board of a packet-boat on one of the lakes. In my younger days I used to allow myself to be stretched upon the Procrustes bed of other people's opinion, though I have got bravely over such folly, and now I generally act, think, and speak as best pleases myself. I slept two glorious nights on the bare turf, with my saddle for a pillow and God's kindly sky for a quilt. I had *heard* of a bed of thorns, of the soft side of a plank, and of the bed-rock. But all my *bodily* experience, theoretical or practical, sinks into insignificance before a bed of cobblestones. Nothing in ancient or modern history can compare with it, unless it be the Irishman's famous down couch, which consisted of a single feather laid upon a rock, and, like him, if it had not been for the name of it, I should have preferred the bare rock. They *said* that there was straw in the ticking upon which we lay, but I should never have imagined so from the feeling. We had neither pillows nor sheets, but the coarsest blue blankets, and not enough of them, for bedclothes; so that we suffered with cold, to add to our other miseries. And then the fleas! Well, like the Grecian artist who veiled the face whose anguish he dared not attempt to depict, I will leave to your imagination that blackest portion of our strange experiences on that awful occasion.

What became of Mr. ——, our host, etc., on this dreadful night, was never known. Mrs. —— and I held council together, and concluded that he was spirited away to some friendly haystack, but as he himself maintained a profound silence on the subject, it remains to this hour an impenetrable mystery, and will be handed down to posterity on the page of history with that of the man in the iron mask, and the more modern but equally insolvable riddle of "Who struck Billy Patterson?"

As soon as it was light we awoke and glanced around the room. On one side hung a large quantity of handsome dresses, with a riding-habit, hat, gauntlets, whip, saddle and bridle, all of the most elegant description. On the other side, a row of shelves contained a number of pans of milk. There was also a very pretty table-service of white crockery, a roll of white carpeting, boxes of soap, chests of tea, casks of sugar, bags of coffee, etc., etc., in the greatest profusion.

We went out into the air. The place, owned by our host, is the most beautiful spot that I ever saw in California. We stood in the midst of a noble grove of the loftiest and largest trees, through which ran two or three carriage-roads, with not a particle of undergrowth to be seen in any direction. Somewhere near the center of this lovely place he is building a house of hewn logs. It will be two stories high, and very large. He intends finishing it with the piazza all around, the first-floor windows to the ground, green blinds, etc. He informed us that he thought it would be finished in three weeks. You can see that it would have been much pleasanter for Mrs. —— to have had the privilege of deferring her visit for a month.

We had a most excellent breakfast. As Mrs. —— said, the good people possessed everything but a house.

Soon after breakfast, my friends, who suspected from appearances the night before that I should not prove a very welcome visitor, came for me, the wife of the proprietor of the American Rancho having good-naturedly retired to the privacy of a covered wagon (she had just crossed the plains) and placed her own room at my disposal. Mrs. —— — insisted upon accompanying me until her friend was better. As she truly said, she was too unwell herself to either assist or amuse another invalid.

My apartment, which was built of logs, was vexatiously small, with no way of letting in light, except by the door. It was as innocent of a floor, and almost as thickly strewn with cobblestones, as the one which I had just left; but then, there *were* some frames built against the side of it, which served for a bedstead, and we had sheets, which, though coarse, were clean. Here, with petticoats, stockings, shoes, and shirts hanging against the logs in picturesque confusion, we received calls from senators, representatives, judges, attorney-generals, doctors, lawyers, officers, editors, and ministers.

The convention came off the day after our arrival in the valley, and as both of the nominees were from our settlement, we began to think that we were quite a people.

Horse-racing and gambling, in all their detestable varieties, were the order of the day. There was faro and poker for the Americans, monte for the Spaniards, lansquenet for the Frenchmen, and smaller games for the outsiders.

At the close of the convention the rancho passed into new hands, and as there was much consequent confusion, I went over to Greenwood's, and Mrs. —— returned to the house of her friend, where, having ordered two or three hundred armfuls of hay to be strewn on the ground, she made a temporary arrangement with some boards for a bedstead, and fell to making sheets from one of the innumerable rolls of cloth which lay about in every direction, for, as I said before, these good people had everything but a house.

My new room, with the exception of its red-calico window, was exactly like the old one. Although it was very small, a man and his wife (the latter was the housekeeper of the establishment) slept there also. With the aid of those everlasting blue blankets I curtained off our part, so as to obtain some small degree of privacy. I had *one* large pocket-handkerchief (it was meant for a young sheet) on my bed, which was filled with good, sweet, fresh hay, and plenty of the azure coverings, so short and narrow that, when once we had lain down, it behooved us to remain perfectly still until morning, as the least movement disarranged the bed-furniture and insured us a shivering night.

On the other side of the partition, against which our bedstead was *built*, stood the cooking-stove, in which they burnt nothing but pitch-pine wood. As the room was not lined, and the boards very loosely put together, the soot sifted through in large quantities and covered us from head to foot, and though I bathed so often that my hands were dreadfully chapped, and bled profusely from having them so much in the water, yet, in spite of my efforts, I looked like a chimney-sweep masquerading in women's clothes.

As it was very cold at this time, the damp ground upon which we were living gave me a severe cough, and I suffered so much from chillness that at last I betook myself to Rob Roy shawls and india-rubbers, and for the rest of the time walked about, a mere bundle of gum elastic and Scotch plaid. My first move in the morning was to go out and sit upon an old traveling wagon which stood in front of my room, in order, like an old beggar-woman, to gather a little warmth from the sun.

Mrs. —— said, "The Bostonians were horror-stricken because the poor Irish, who had never known any other mode of living, had no floors in their cabins, and were getting up all sorts of Howard benevolent societies to supply unfortunate Pat with what is to him an unwished-for luxury." She thought that they would be much better employed in organizing associations for ameliorating the condition of those wretched women in California who were so mad as to leave their comfortable homes in the mines to go a-pleasuring in the valleys.

My poor husband suffered even more than I did, for though he had a nominal share in my luxurious bed with its accompanying pocket-handkerchief, yet, as Mrs. —— took it into her head to pay me a visit, he was obliged to resign it to her and betake himself to the barroom, and as every bunk and all the blankets were engaged, he was compelled to lie on the bar-floor (thank Heaven, there was a civilized floor there, of real boards), with his boots for a pillow.

But I am sure you must be tired of this long letter, for I am, and I reserve the rest of my adventures in the American Valley until another time.

Letter the Twenty-second

[The Pioneer, November, 1855]

The OVERLAND TIDE of IMMIGRATION

SYNOPSIS

Exoneration of landlords for conditions at Greenwood's Rancho. The American Valley. Prospective summer resort. Prodigious vegetables. New England scenery compared with that of California. Greenwood's Rancho. Place of origin of quartz hoax. Beautiful stones. Recruiting-place of overland immigrants. Haggard immigrant women. Death and speedy burial on the plains. Handsome young widow immigrant. Aspirants to matrimony candidates for her hand. Interesting stories of adventures on the plains. Four women, sisters or sisters-in-law, and their thirty-six children. Accomplished men. Infant prodigies. A widow with eight sons and one daughter. Primitive laundering, but generous patrons. The bloomer costume appropriate for overland journey. Dances in barroom. Unwilling female partners. Some illiterate immigrants. Many intelligent and well-bred women. The journey back to Indian Bar. The tame frog in the rancho barroom. The dining-table a bed at night. Elation of the author on arriving at her own log cabin.

Letter the Twenty-second
The Overland Tide of Immigration
From our Log Cabin, Indian Bar,
October 27, 1852.

In my last epistle, my dear M., I left myself safely ensconced at Greenwood's Rancho, in about as uncomfortable a position as a person could well be, where board was fourteen dollars a week. Now, you must not think that the proprietors were at all to blame for our miserable condition. They were, I assure you, very gentlemanly and intelligent men, and I owe them a thousand thanks for the many acts of kindness and the friendly efforts which they made to amuse and interest me while I was in their house. They said from the first that they were utterly unprepared to receive ladies, and it was only after some persuasion, and as a favor to me, that they consented to let me come. They intend soon to build a handsome house, for it is thought that this valley will be a favorite summer resort for people from the cities below.

The American Valley is one of the most beautiful in all California. It is seven miles long and three or four wide, with the Feather River wending its quiet way through it, unmolested by flumes and undisturbed by wing-dams. It is a superb farming country, everything growing in the greatest luxuriance. I saw turnips there which measured larger round than my waist, and all other vegetables in the same proportion. There are beautiful rides in every direction, though I was too unwell during my stay there to explore them as I wished. There is one drawback upon the beauty of these valleys, and it is one peculiar to all the scenery in this part of California, and that is, the monotonous tone of the foliage, nearly all the trees being firs. One misses that infinite variety of waving forms, and those endless shades of verdure, which make New England forest scenery so exquisitely lovely. And then that gorgeous autumnal phenomenon, witnessed, I believe, nowhere but in the Northern States of the Union, one never sees here. How often, in my far-away Yankee home, have I laid me down at eve, with the whole earth looking so freshly green, to rise in the morning and behold the wilderness blossoming, not only like the rose, but like all other flowers besides, and glittering as if a shower of butterflies had fallen upon it during the silent watches of the night. I have a vague idea that I "hooked" that butterfly comparison from somebody. If so, I beg the injured person's pardon, and he or she may have a hundred of *mine* to pay for it.

It was at Greenwood's Rancho that the famous quartz hoax originated last winter, which so completely gulled our good miners on the river. I visited the spot, which has been excavated to some extent. The stone is very beautiful, being lined and streaked and splashed with crimson, purple, green, orange, and black. There was one large white block, veined with stripes of a magnificent blood-red color, and partly covered with a dark mass, which was the handsomest thing of the kind I ever saw. Some of the crystallizations were wonderfully perfect. I had a piece of the bed-rock given me, completely covered with natural prisms varying in size from an inch down to those not larger than the head of a pin.

Much of the immigration from across the plains, on its way to the cities below, stops here for a while to recruit. I always had a strange fancy for that nomadic way of coming to California. To lie down under starry skies, hundreds of miles from any human habitation, and to rise up on dewy mornings to pursue our way through a strange country, so wildly beautiful, seeing each day something new and wonderful, seemed to me truly enchanting. But cruel reality strips *everything* of its rose tints. The poor women arrive looking as haggard as so many Endorian witches, burnt to the color of a hazelnut, with their hair cut short, and its gloss entirely destroyed by the alkali, whole plains of which they are compelled to cross on the way. You will hardly find a family that has not left some beloved one buried upon the plains. And they are fearful funerals, those. A person dies, and they stop just long enough to dig his grave and lay him in it as decently as circumstances will permit, and the long train hurries onward, leaving its healthy companion of yesterday, perhaps, in this boundless city of the dead. On this hazardous journey they dare not linger.

I was acquainted with a young widow of twenty, whose husband died of cholera when they were but five weeks on their journey. He was a judge in one of the Western States, and a man of some eminence in his profession. She is a pretty little creature, and all the aspirants to matrimony are candidates for her hand.

One day a party of immigrant women came into my room, which was also the parlor of the establishment. Some observation was made, which led me to inquire of one of them if her husband was with her.

"She hain't got no husband," fairly *chuckled* one of her companions. "She came with *me*, and her feller died of cholera on the plains."

At this startling and brutal announcement the poor girl herself gave a hysteric giggle, which I at first thought proceeded from heartlessness, but I was told afterwards, by the person under whose immediate protection she came out, and who was a sister of her betrothed, that the tender woman's heart received such a fearful shock at the sudden death of her lover, that for several weeks her life was despaired of.

I spent a great deal of time calling at the different encampments, for nothing enchanted me half so much as to hear about this strange exodus from the States. I never weary of listening to stories of adventures on the plains, and some of the family histories are deeply interesting.

I was acquainted with four women, all sisters or sisters-in-law, who had among them thirty-six children, the entire number of which had arrived thus far in perfect health. They could, of themselves, form quite a respectable village.

The immigration this year contained many intelligent and truly elegant persons, who, having caught the fashionable epidemic, had left luxurious homes in the States to come to California. Among others, there was a young gentleman of nineteen, the son of a United

States Senator, who, having just graduated, felt adventurous, and determined to cross the plains. Like the rest, he arrived in a somewhat dilapidated condition, with elbows out, and a hat the very counterpart of Sam Weller' s "gossamer ventilation," which, if you remember, "though *not* a very handsome 'un to look at, was an astonishin' good 'un to wear!" I must confess that he became ragged clothes the best of any one I ever saw, and made me think of the picturesque beggar boys in Murillo's paintings of Spanish life.

Then there was a person who used to sing in public with Ossian Dodge. He had a voice of remarkable purity and sweetness, which he was kind enough to permit us to hear now and then. I hardly know of what nation he claimed to be. His father was an Englishman, his mother an Italian. He was born in Poland, and had lived nearly all his life in the United States. He was not the only musical genius that we had among us. There was a little girl at one of the tents who had taught herself to play on the accordion on the way out. She was really quite a prodigy, singing very sweetly, and accompanying herself with much skill upon the instrument.

There was another child, whom I used to go to look at as I would go to examine a picture. She had, without exception, the most beautiful face I ever saw. Even the alkali had not been able to mar the golden glory of the curls which clustered around that splendid little head. She had soft brown eyes, which shone from beneath their silken lashes like "a tremulous evening star"; a mouth which made you think of a string of pearls threaded on scarlet; and a complexion of the waxen purity of the japonica, with the exception of a band of brownest freckles, which, extending from the tip of each cheek straight across the prettiest possible nose, added, I used to fancy, a new beauty to her enchanting face. She was very fond of me, and used to bring me wild cherries which her brothers had gathered for her. Many a morning I have raised my eyes from my book, startled by that vision of infant loveliness—for her step had the still grace of a snow-flake—standing in beautiful silence by my side.

But the most interesting of all my pets was a widow whom we used to call the "long woman." When but a few weeks on the journey, she had buried her husband, who died of cholera after about six hours' illness. She had come on; for what else could she do? No one was willing to guide her back to her old home in the States, and when I knew her she was living under a large tree a few rods from the rancho, and sleeping at night, with all her family, in her one covered wagon. God only knows where they all stowed themselves away, for she was a modern Mrs. Rogers, with "nine small children and one at the breast." Indeed, of this catechismal number the oldest was but fifteen years of age, and the youngest a nursing babe of six months. She had eight sons and one daughter. Just fancy how dreadful! Only one girl to all that boy! People used to wonder what took me so often to her encampment, and at the interest with which I listened to what they called her stupid talk. Certainly there was nothing poetical about the woman. Leigh Hunt's friend could not have elevated *her* commonplace into the sublime. She was immensely tall, and had a hard, weather-beaten face, surmounted by a dreadful horn comb and a heavy twist of hay-colored hair, which, before it was cut, and its gloss all destroyed by the alkali, must, from its luxuriance, have been very handsome. But what really interested me so much in her was the dogged and determined way in which she had set that stern, wrinkled face of hers against poverty. She owned nothing in the world but her team, and yet she planned all sorts of successful ways to get food for her small, or rather large, family. She used to wash shirts, and iron them on a chair, in the open air of course, and you can fancy with what success. But the gentlemen were too generous to be critical, and as they paid her three or four times as much as she asked, she accumulated quite a handsome sum in a few days. She made me think of a long-legged very thin hen scratching for dear life to feed her never-to-be-satisfied brood. Poor woman! She told me that she was compelled to allowance *her* young ones, and that she seldom gave them as much as they could eat at any one meal. She was worse off than the

old woman who lived in a shoe,
And had so many children she didn't know what to do.
To some she gave butter, to some she gave bread,
And to some she gave whippings, and sent them to bed.

Now, *my* old woman had no butter, and very little bread; and she was so naturally economical that even whippings were sparingly administered. But, after all their privations, they were, with the exception of the eldest hope, as healthy-looking a set of ragged little wretches as ever I saw. The aforesaid "hope" was the longest, the leanest, and the bob-sidedest specimen of a Yankee that it is possible to imagine. He wore a white face, whiter eyes, and whitest hair, and walked about looking as if existence was the merest burden and he wished somebody would have the goodness to take it off his hands. He seemed always to be in the act of yoking up a pair of oxen, and ringing every change of which the English alphabet is capable upon the one single Yankee execration, "Darnation!" which he scattered, in all its comical varieties, upon the tow head of his young brother, a piece of chubby giggle, who was forever trying to hold up a dreadful yoke, which *wouldn't* "stay put," in spite of all the efforts of those fat dirty little hands of his. The "long woman," mother-like, excused him by saying that he had been sick, though once, when the "Darned fools" flew thicker than usual, she gently observed that he had forgotten that he was a child himself once. He certainly retained no trace of having enjoyed that delightful state of existence, and though one would not be so rude as to call him an old boy, yet, being always clad in a middle-aged habit, an elderly coat, and adult pantaloons, one would as little fancy him a *young* man. Perhaps the fact of his wearing his father's wardrobe in all its unaltered amplitude might help to confuse one's ideas on the subject.

There was another dear old lady to whom I took the largest kind of a liking, she was so exquisitely neat. Although she too had no floor, her babe always had on a clean white dress, and face to match. She was about four feet high, and had a perfect passion for wearing those frightful frontpieces of false hair with which the young women of L. were once in the habit of covering their abundant tresses. She used to send me little pots of fresh butter,—the first that I had tasted since I left the States,—beautifully stamped, and looking like ingots of virgin gold. I, of course, made a dead-set at the frontpiece, though I do believe that to this distorted taste, and its accompanying horror of a cap, she owed the preservation of her own beautiful hair. To please me she laid it aside, but I am convinced that it was restored to its proud eminence as soon as I left the valley, for she evidently had a "sneaking kindness" for it that nothing could destroy. I have sometimes thought that she wore it from religious principle, thinking it her duty to look as old as possible, for she appeared fifteen years younger when she took it off. She told me that in crossing the plains she used to stop on Saturdays, and taking everything out of the wagons, wash them in strong lye, to which precaution she attributed the perfect health which they all enjoyed (the *family*, not the wagons) during the whole journey.

There is one thing for which the immigrants deserve high praise, and that is, for having adopted the bloomer dress (frightful as it is on all other occasions) in crossing the plains. For such an excursion it is just the thing.

I ought to say a word about the dances which we used to have in the barroom, a place so low that a *very* tall man could not have stood upright in it. One side was fitted up as a store, and another side with bunks for lodgers. These bunks were elegantly draperied with red calico, through which we caught dim glimpses of blue blankets. If they could only have had sheets, they would have fairly been enveloped in the American colors. By the way, I wonder if there is anything *national* in this eternal passion for blue blankets and red calico. On ball-nights the bar was closed, and everything was very quiet and respectable. To be sure, there was some danger of being swept away in a flood of tobacco-juice, but luckily the floor was uneven, and it lay around in puddles, which with care one could avoid, merely running the minor risk of falling prostrate upon the wet boards in the midst of a galopade.

Of course the company was made up principally of the immigrants. Such dancing, such dressing, and such conversation, surely was never heard or seen before. The gentlemen generally were compelled to have a regular fight with their fair partners before they could drag them onto the floor. I am happy to say that almost always the stronger vessel won the day, or rather night, except in the case of certain timid youths, who, after one or two attacks, gave up the battle in despair.

I thought that I had had some experience in bad grammar since I came to California, but these good people were the first that I had ever heard use right royal *we* instead of *us*. Do not imagine that all, or even the larger part, of the company were of this description. There were many intelligent and well-bred women, whose acquaintance I made with extreme pleasure.

After reading the description of the inconveniences and discomforts which we suffered in the American Valley,—and I can assure you that I have not at all exaggerated them,—you may imagine my joy when two of our friends arrived from Indian Bar for the purpose of accompanying us home. We took two days for our return, and thus I was not at all fatigued. The weather was beautiful, our friends amusing, and F. well and happy. We stopped at night at a rancho where they had a tame frog. You cannot think how comic it looked hopping about the bar, quite as much at home as a tame squirrel would have been. I had a bed made up for me at this place, on one end of a long dining-table. It was very comfortable, with the trifling drawback that I had to rise earlier than I wished, in order that what had been a bed at night might become a table by day.

We stopped at the top of the hill and set fire to some fir-trees. Oh, how splendidly they looked, with the flames leaping and curling amid the dark green foliage like a golden snake fiercely beautiful. The shriek which the fire gave as it sprang upon its verdant prey made me think of the hiss of some furious reptile about to wrap in its burning folds its helpless victim.

With what perfect delight did I re-enter my beloved log cabin. One of our good neighbors had swept and put it in order before my arrival, and everything was as clean and neat as possible. How grateful to my feet felt the thick warm carpet; how perfect appeared the floor, which I had once reviled (I begged its pardon on the spot) because it was not exactly even; how cozy the old faded-calico couch; how thoroughly comfortable the four chairs (two of them had been thoroughly rebottomed with brown sail-cloth, tastefully put on, with a border of carpet-tacks); how truly elegant the closet-case toilet-table, with the doll's looking-glass hanging above, which showed my face (the first time that I had seen it since I left home) some six shades darker than usual; how convenient the trunk, which did duty as a wash-stand, with its vegetable-dish instead of a bowl (at the rancho I had a pint tin pan when it was not in use in the kitchen); but, above and beyond all, how superbly luxurious the magnificent bedstead, with its splendid hair mattress, its clean, wide linen sheets, its nice square pillows, and its large, generous blankets and quilts. And then the cozy little supper, arrayed on a table-cloth, and the long, delightful evening afterwards, by a fragrant fire of beech and pine, when we talked over our past sufferings. Oh, it was delicious as a dream, and almost made amends for the three dreadful weeks of pleasuring in the American Valley.

Letter the Twenty-third

[The Pioneer, December, 1855]

MINING FAILURES—DEPARTURE from INDIAN BAR

SYNOPSIS

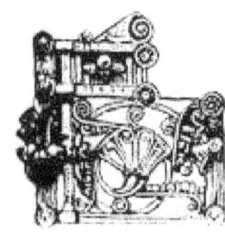

Dread of spending another winter at Indian Bar. Failure of nearly all the fluming companies. Official report of one company. Incidental failure of business people. The author's preparations to depart. Prediction of early rains. High prices cause of dealers' failure to lay in supply of provisions. Probable fatal results to families unable to leave Bar. Rain and snow. The Squire a poor weather prophet. Pack-mule trains with provisions fail to arrive. Amusement found in petty litigation. Legal acumen of the Squire. He wins golden opinions. The judgment all the prevailing party gets. What the constable got in effort to collect judgment. Why Dr. C.'s fee was not paid. A prescription of "calumny and other pizen doctor's stuff". A wonderful gold specimen in the form of a basket. "Weighs about two dollars and a half". How little it takes to make people comfortable. A log-cabin meal and its table-service. The author departs on horseback from Indian Bar. Her regrets upon leaving the mountains. "Feeble, half-dying invalid not recognizable in your now perfectly healthy sister."

Letter the Twenty-third
Mining Failures—Departure from Indian Bar
From our Log Cabin, Indian Bar,
November 21, 1852.

I suppose, Molly dear,—at least, I flatter myself,—that you have been wondering and fretting a good deal for the last few weeks at not hearing from Dame Shirley. The truth is, that I have been wondering and fretting *myself* almost into a fever at the dreadful prospect of being compelled to spend the winter here, which, on every account, is undesirable.

To our unbounded surprise, we found, on our return from the American Valley, that nearly all the fluming companies had failed. Contrary to every expectation, on arriving at the bed-rock no gold made its appearance. But a short history of the rise, progress, and final fate of one of these associations, given me in writing by its own secretary, conveys a pretty correct idea of the result of the majority of the remainder.

"The thirteen men, of which the American Fluming Company consisted, commenced getting out timber in February. On the 5th of July they began to lay the flume. A thousand dollars were paid for lumber which they were compelled to buy. They built a dam six feet high and three hundred feet in length, upon which thirty men labored nine days and a half. The cost of said dam was estimated at two thousand dollars. This company left off working on the twenty-fourth day of September, having taken out, in *all*, gold-dust to the amount of forty-one dollars and seventy cents! Their lumber and tools, sold at auction, brought about two hundred dollars."

A very small amount of arithmetical knowledge will enable one to figure up what the American Fluming Company made by *their* summer's work. This result was by no means a singular one. Nearly every person on the river received the same stepmother's treatment from Dame Nature in this her mountain workshop.

Of course the whole world (*our* world) was, to use a phrase much in vogue here, "dead broke." The shopkeepers, restaurants, and gambling-houses, with an amiable confidingness peculiar to such people, had trusted the miners to that degree that they themselves were in the same moneyless condition. Such a batch of woeful faces was never seen before, not the least elongated of which was F.'s, to whom nearly all the companies owed large sums.

Of course with the failure of the golden harvest Othello's occupation was gone. The mass of the unfortunates laid down the shovel and the hoe, and left the river in crowds. It is said that there are not twenty men remaining on Indian Bar, although two months ago you could count them up by hundreds.

We were to have departed on the 5th of November, and my toilet-table and wash-hand-stand, duly packed for that occasion, their occupation *also* gone, have remained ever since in the humble position of mere trunks. To be sure, the expressman called for us at the appointed time, but, unfortunately, F. had not returned from the American Valley, where he had gone to visit a sick friend, and Mr. Jones was not willing to wait even one day, so much did he fear being caught in a snowstorm with his mules. It was the general opinion, from unmistakable signs, that the rainy season would set in a month earlier than common, and with unusual severity. Our friends urged me to start on with Mr. Jones and some other acquaintances, and leave F. to follow on foot, as he could easily overtake us in a few hours. This I decidedly refused to do, preferring to run the fearful risk of being compelled to spend the winter in the mountains, which, as there is not enough flour to last six weeks, and we personally have not laid in a pound of provisions, is not so indifferent a matter as it may at first appear to you. The traders have delayed getting in their winter stock, on account of the high price of flour, and God only knows how fatal may be the result of this selfish delay to the unhappy mountaineers, many of whom, having families here, are unable to escape into the valley.

It is the twenty-first day of November, and for the last three weeks it has rained and snowed alternately, with now and then a fair day sandwiched between, for the express purpose, as it has seemed, of aggravating our misery, for, after twelve hours of such sunshine as only our own California can show, we were sure to be gratified by an exceedingly well got up tableau of the deluge, *without* that ark of safety, a mule team, which, sister-Anna-like, we were ever straining our eyes to see descending the hill. "There! I hear a mule-bell," would be the cry at least a dozen times a day, when away we would all troop to the door, to behold nothing but great brown raindrops rushing merrily downward, as if in mockery of our sufferings. Five times did the Squire, who has lived for some two or three years in the mountains, and is quite weather-wise, solemnly affirm that the rain was over for the present, and five times did the storm-torrent of the next morning give our prophet the lie. In the mean while we have been expecting, each day, the advent of a mule train. Now the rumor goes that Clark's mules have arrived at Pleasant Valley, and now that Bob Lewis's train has reached the Wild Yankee's, or that Jones, with any quantity of animals and provisions, has been seen on the brow of the hill, and will probably get in by evening. Thus constantly is alternating light and gloom in a way that nearly drives me mad.

The few men that have remained on the Bar have amused themselves by prosecuting one another right and left. The Squire, bless his honest, lazy, Leigh Huntish face, comes out strong on these occasions. He has pronounced decisions which, for legal acumen, brilliancy, and acuteness, would make Daniel Webster, could he hear them, tear his hair to that extent—from sheer envy—that he would be compelled to have a wig ever after. But, jesting apart, the Squire's course has been so fair, candid, and sensible, that he has won golden opinions from all; and were it not for his insufferable laziness and good nature, he would have made a most excellent justice of the peace. The prosecuting party generally "gets judgment," which is about all he *does* get, though sometimes the constable is more fortunate, as happened to-day to our friend W., who, having been detained on the Bar by the rain, got himself sworn into the above office for the fun of the thing. He performs his duties with great delight, and is always accompanied by a guard of honor, consisting of the majority of the men remaining in the place. He entered the cabin about one hour ago, when the following spicy conversation took place between him and F., who happened to be the prosecutor in this day's proceedings.

"Well, old fellow, did you see Big Bill?" eagerly inquired F.

"Yes," is the short and sullen reply.

"And what did you *get*?" continued his questioner.

"I got THIS!" savagely shouts the amateur constable, at the same time pointing with a grin of rage to a huge swelling on his upper lip, gleaming with all the colors of the rainbow.

"What did you do then?" was the next meek inquiry.

"Oh, I came away," says our brave young officer of justice. And indeed it would have been madness to have resisted this delightful Big Bill, who stands six feet four inches in his stockings, with a corresponding amount of bone and muscle, and is a star of the first magnitude in boxing circles. F. saved the creature's life last winter, having watched with him three nights in succession. He refuses to pay his bill "'cos he gin him *calumny* and other pizen doctor's stuff." Of course poor W. got dreadfully laughed at, though I looked as solemn as possible while I stayed him with cups of coffee, comforted him with beefsteaks and onions, and coaxed the wounded upper lip with an infinite succession of little bits of brown paper drowned in brandy.

I wish that you could see *me* about these times. I am generally found seated on a cigar-box in the chimney-corner, my chin in my hand, rocking backwards and forwards (weaving, you used to call it) in a despairing way, and now and then casting a picturesquely hopeless glance about our dilapidated cabin. Such a looking place as it is! Not having been repaired, the rain, pouring down the outside of the chimney, which is inside of the house, has liquefied the mud, which now lies in spots all over the splendid tin mantelpiece, and festoons itself in graceful arabesques along the sides thereof. The lining overhead is dreadfully stained, the rose-garlanded hangings are faded and torn, the sofa-covering displays picturesque glimpses of hay, and the poor, old, worn-out carpet is not enough to make india-rubbers desirable.

Sometimes I lounge forlornly to the window and try to take a bird's-eye view of outdoors. First, now a large pile of gravel prevents my seeing anything else, but by dint of standing on tiptoe I catch sight of a hundred other large piles of gravel, Pelion-upon-Ossa-like heaps of gigantic stones, excavations of fearful deepness, innumerable tents, calico hovels, shingle palaces, ramadas (pretty arbor-like places, composed of green boughs, and baptized with that sweet name), half a dozen blue and red shirted miners, and one hatless hombre, in garments of the airiest description, reclining gracefully at the entrance of the Humboldt in that transcendental state of intoxication when a man is compelled to hold on to the earth for fear of falling off. The whole Bar is thickly peppered with empty bottles, oyster-cans, sardine-boxes, and brandied-fruit jars, the harsher outlines of which are softened off by the thinnest possible coating of radiant snow. The river, freed from its wooden-flume prison, rolls gracefully by. The green and purple beauty of these majestic old mountains looks lovelier than ever, through its pearl-like network of foaming streamlets, while, like an immense concave of pure sapphire without spot or speck, the wonderful and never-enough-to-be-talked-about sky of California drops down upon the whole its fathomless splendor. The day happens to be the inner fold of one of the atmospheric sandwiches alluded to above. Had it been otherwise, I doubt whether I should have had spirit enough to write to you.

I have just been called from my letter to look at a wonderfully curious gold specimen. I will try to describe it to you; and to convince you that I do not exaggerate its rare beauty, I must inform you that two friends of ours have each offered a hundred dollars for it, and a blacksmith in the place—a man utterly unimaginative, who would not throw away a red cent on a *mere* fancy—has tried to purchase it for fifty dollars. I wish most earnestly that you could see it. It is of unmixed gold, weighing about two dollars and a half. Your first idea on looking at it is of an exquisite little basket. There is the graceful cover with its rounded nub at the top, the three finely carved sides (it is triformed), the little stand upon which it sets, and the tiny clasp which fastens it. In detail it is still more beautiful. On one side you see a perfect W, each finely shaded bar of which is fashioned with the nicest exactness. The second surface presents to view a Grecian profile, whose delicately cut features remind you of the serene beauty of an antique gem. It is surprising how much expression this face contains, which is enriched by an oval setting of delicate beading. A plain triangular space of burnished gold, surrounded with bead-work similar to that which outlines the profile, seems left on purpose for a name. The owner, who is a Frenchman, decidedly refuses to sell this gem, and you will probably never have an opportunity to see that the same Being who has commanded the violet to be beautiful can fashion the gold, crucibled into metallic purity within the earth's dark heart, into shapes as lovely and curious.

To my extreme vexation, Ned, that jewel of cooks and fiddlers, departed at the first approach of rain, since when I have been obliged to take up the former delightful employment myself. Really, everybody ought to go to the mines, just to see how little it takes to make people comfortable in the world. My ordinary utensils consist of,—item, one iron dipper, which holds exactly three pints; item, one brass kettle of the same size; and item, the gridiron, made out of an old shovel, which I described in a former letter. With these three assistants I perform absolute wonders in the culinary way. Unfortunately, I am generally compelled to get three breakfasts, for sometimes the front-stick *will* break, and then down comes the brass kettle of potatoes and the dipper of coffee, extinguishing the fire, spilling the breakfast, wetting the carpet, scalding the dog, waking up F. from an eleven-o'clock-in-the-day dream, and compelling poor me to get up a second edition of my morning's work on safer and more scientific principles.

At dinner-time some good-natured friend carves the beef at a stove outside, on condition that he may have a plate and knife and fork at our table. So when that meal is ready I spread on the said table, which at other times does duty as a china-closet, a quarter of a sheet, which, with its three companion quarters, was sanctified and set apart, when I first arrived here, for that sacred purpose. As our guests generally amount to six or eight, we dispense the three teaspoons at the rate of one to every two or three persons. All sorts of outlandish dishes serve as teacups. Among others, wine-glasses and tumblers—there are always plenty of these in the mines—figure largely. Last night, our company being larger than usual, one of our friends was compelled to take his tea out of a soup-plate. The same individual, not being able to find a seat, went outside and brought in an empty gin-cask, upon which he sat, sipping iron tablespoonfuls of his tea, in great apparent glory and contentment.

F. has just entered, with the joyful news that the expressman has arrived. He says that it will be impossible for mule trains to get in for some time to come, even if the storm is really over, which he does not believe. In many places on the mountains the snow is already five feet in depth, although he thinks that, so many people are constantly leaving for the valley, the path will be kept open, so that I can make the journey with comparative ease on his horse, which he has kindly offered to lend me, volunteering to accompany F., and some others who will make their exodus at the same time, on foot. Of course I shall be obliged to leave my trunks, merely taking a change of linen in a carpet bag. We shall leave to-morrow, whether it rain or snow, for it would be madness to linger any longer.

My heart is heavy at the thought of departing forever from this place. I *like* this wild and barbarous life. I leave it with regret. The solemn fir-trees, whose "slender tops *are* close against the sky" here, the watching hills, and the calmly beautiful river, seem to gaze sorrowfully at me as I stand in the moonlighted midnight to bid them farewell. Beloved, unconventional wood-life; divine Nature, into whose benign eyes I never looked, whose many voices, gay and glad, I never heard, in the artificial heart of the busy world,—I quit your serene teachings for a restless and troubled future. Yes, Molly, smile if you will at my folly, but I go from the mountains with a deep heart-sorrow. I took kindly to this existence, which to you seems so sordid and mean. Here, at least, I have been contented. The "thistle-seed," as you call me, sent abroad its roots right lovingly into this barren soil, and gained an unwonted strength in what seemed to you such unfavorable surroundings. You would hardly recognize the feeble and half-dying invalid, who drooped languidly out of sight as night shut down between your straining gaze and the good ship Manilla as she wafted her far away from her Atlantic home, in the person of your *now* perfectly healthy sister.

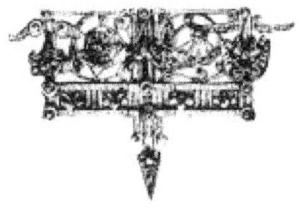

Lightning Source UK Ltd.
Milton Keynes UK
UKHW040015060620
364507UK00001B/148